Beyond Together or Apart

Planning for, assessing and placing sibling groups

Shelagh Beckett

coramBAAF
ADOPTION & FOSTERING ACADEMY

Published by
CoramBAAF Adoption and Fostering Academy
41 Brunswick Square
London WC1N 1AZ
www.corambaaf.org.uk

Coram Academy Limited, registered as a company limited by guarantee in England and Wales number 9697712, part of the Coram group, charity number 312278

© Shelagh Beckett 2018, 2021
Second edition 2021

British Library Cataloguing in Publication Data
A catalogue record for this book is available from the British Library

ISBN 978 1 913384 07 4

Project management by Jo Francis, CoramBAAF
Designed and typeset by Helen Joubert Design
Printed in Great Britain by The Lavenham Press

All rights reserved. Apart from any fair dealing for the purposes of research or private study, or criticism or review, as permitted under the Copyright, Designs and Patents Act 1988, this publication may not be reproduced, stored in a retrieval system, or transmitted in any form or by any means, without the prior written permission of the publishers.

The moral right of the author has been asserted in accordance with the Copyright, Designs and Patents Act 1988.

✉ For the latest news on CoramBAAF titles and special offers, sign up to our free publications bulletin at https://corambaaf.org.uk/subscribe.

Contents

1	**Introduction**	**1**
	A charter for brothers and sisters	6
	Core values and principles	7
	How to make best use of this guide	8
2	**Children's sibling relationships: what helps or hinders them?**	**10**
	Introduction	10
	Children's relationships with brothers and sisters	10
	The impact of early family life, parenting, emotional warmth and differential treatment	13
	Adverse childhood experiences and sibling relationships	15
	The impact of domestic violence, fear and uncertainty	16
	Bullying and peer and sibling relationships	18
	Caregiving behaviours	19
	Disability	20
	Links between friendships and sibling relationships	20
	Research – improving sibling relationships	21
	Key points	22
3	**Becoming looked after: early planning, placement and contact for brothers and sisters**	**24**
	Introduction	24
	Children and young people – what matters to them	24
	Research – placement together in foster care	26
	Early planning and placing children	28
	Foster families	30
	Intervening to help promote better peer and sibling relationships – what might help?	35
	Foster carers and separated siblings – placement and contact issues	36
	Key practice points	38
	Work with the children – photos, explanations and visits	39
	Key practice points	40

The quality of contact/family time – observations and links to assessment	40
Key practice points	41
Key messages	42

4 Frameworks for the assessment of sibling relationships and placements — 44

Introduction	44
Various frameworks, models and approaches	44
Discussion – frameworks	51
Key practice points	51

5 Assessment: what you should include and why — 53

Introduction	53
Assessment: key elements and rationale	55
Structuring and managing the process – what a coherent assessment might include	57
Understanding needs and behaviours – incorporating SDQs into your assessment	66
Discussion and practice points	68
Analysis	69
Circumstances that may indicate that siblings should be placed separately	70
Identifying who should be placed with whom and considering permanence options	72
Making decisions	73
Recording – the importance of clear written explanations for children and their families	75
Key practice points	76

6 Involving children, providing explanations and doing life story work — 77

Introduction	77
Explanations and life story work	85
Key practice points	87

7 Recruiting and preparing new families — 88

Introduction	88
Recruiting permanent new families	88
Preparing, assessing and approving families	91
Key aspects to explore and address in adoption assessments	94
The impact on existing children	96

Support within the adopters' network and beyond	96
Training, preparation and the adoption panel	96
Key practice points	97

8 Preparing to move, matching and introductions — 99
Introduction	99
Sharing information	99
Introductions – paying attention to children's and adults' emotional needs	101
Adopters and foster carers – their relationship and needs	104
Planning moves	109
Moving in all together or not?	112
Children in separate placements and where continued placement apart is planned	113
Children currently placed together who are to go to separate permanent families	114
Key practice points	115

9 Brothers and sisters: visits and keeping in touch — 116
Planning and supporting contact	117
Planning contact – pointers from research	119
Key points	122
Contact between adopted children and siblings in long-term foster care/with family members	122
Is there too much focus on risk and not enough on benefits?	123
Specialist organisations helping siblings to meet up	124
Key practice points	125

10 Research: how children and their families fare — 127
Introduction	127
Overview – children's family backgrounds, their pre-placement experiences and needs	127
Introductions and the early days	128
The "care-giver" child	129
Children's sibling and peer relationships	130
Aggression, emotional regulation and sibling conflicts	131
Summary of key research findings	132

11 Planning the right support for children and families — 133
Introduction	133
Helping birth children and placed children to get along	134

Research on post-placement support	135
Adoption Support Fund	136
Planning support	136
Summary	142
Key practice points	143

Conclusions — 144

References — 148

Appendices — 157

Appendix 1: Overview of legislation, guidance and NICE/SCIE guidance	158
Appendix 2: Forms and sample letters	167
Appendix 3: Useful reading and online resources	189
Appendix 4: Adopters' accounts	193

FORMS AVAILABLE FOR PURCHASE

The forms and sample letters in Appendix 2 are available here for agencies to copy, amend and use as they wish. All of these forms and sample letters are also available as Word templates for purchase; the set of forms costs £25.00 plus VAT = £30.00. These can be purchased, for unlimited future use, at: www.corambaaf.org.uk/bookshop, or by contacting CoramBAAF Publications Sales at pubs.sales@corambaaf.org.uk or on 020 7520 7517.

Acknowledgements

I would like to thank Sarah Borthwick and Elaine Dibben for reading the first draft, and for their encouragement and thoughtful suggestions. Dr John Simmonds and Elaine Dibben, from CoramBAAF, and Professor Julie Selwyn, from the University of Bristol, highlighted or shared relevant research and I am grateful to each of them. The contribution of Professor Dieter Wolke (University of Warwick) was also important in helping me to better understand the links between sibling and peer bullying.

Alexandra Conroy Harris from CoramBAAF assisted with the section on law and guidance. Shaila Shah and Jo Francis were not only patient editors but also allowed me the freedom to write a much wider text than they had initially envisaged.

Foster carers and adoptive parents were unstintingly generous in responding to my requests: sharing their experiences and taking time to put pen to paper or, more accurately, fingers to keyboards. Some of them did so late at night when their children were, at long last, asleep. This guide is, I think, richer as a result of what they all added – thank you.

At the core of this book is a focus on relationships and the need for them to be truly valued. Two colleagues who became wonderful and hugely caring best friends deserve a special mention: Fran Ward and Chris Smith. Last, but not least, Dr Brian Lloyd, whose love and care knows no bounds.

Note about the author

Shelagh Beckett has extensive experience as a practitioner and manager specialising in children's services, adoption and fostering. She now provides independent consultancy and training to local authorities, the third sector and the media. For many years, Shelagh has undertaken expert witness assessments – often in respect of brothers and sisters – and has taught on child care courses. She also provides consultancy on documentaries that feature children, children's services or charities; these have included award-winning television programmes on child protection, fostering, adoption and bereavement.

Shelagh has previously written chapters in various publications – some of which have focused on the needs of looked after and adopted brothers and sisters.

Chapter 1
Introduction

Brothers and sisters who share a childhood and grow up together have potentially the longest lasting, and one of the closest, relationships of their lives with each other. In common with all relationships, sibling relationships have enormous capacity for shared understanding and activity, can stimulate warmth, care and joy, and can help to sustain children and adults through distressing times. They also have the potential to be undermining, riven by conflict and marred by difficulty. Whilst these qualities are evident in most relationships, there are also differences and unique aspects of sibling interactions that are important to understand, think about and address when working with looked after children. Even when a child has never lived with his or her sibling/s, the significance of the relationship may be keenly felt during childhood with a sense of "what might have been" stretching into adult life.

"Sibling" is a convenient shorthand term and is used in this guide; much research and other guidance also use this term. However, this guide is about brothers and sisters and this description is preferred. It is more powerful and means more to most people and has therefore been used as much as possible.

In 2008, when an earlier edition of this guide was last published, the timescale for court proceedings was substantially longer. The Family Justice Review (2011) set out that care cases were taking on average over a year, with considerable variation between different areas. In July 2013, revised procedures, called the Public Law Outline, were introduced with the aim of completing care proceedings within 26 weeks. Since this introduction, timescales have reduced significantly but remain challenging, most especially for the children involved. Assessments of sibling relationships are now required earlier and the way in which this work is planned merits fresh focus.

Over the past decade, our knowledge about sibling relationships and the impact of multiple adversities experienced in childhood has also grown, though attention and priority continue to be accorded far more readily to adult–child relationships. Many reports – over many years – have exhorted us to listen to the voices and experiences of children and young people. Nowhere is this more needed than in respect of siblings. Children and young people have much to tell us about the importance of brothers and sisters in their lives.

In a mixed-methods study of sibling contact in England and Wales, Monk and Macvarish (2018, p. 2) set out that:

> *Routine decision making in the Family Courts can have a significant impact on children and young people's sibling relationships. The impact is most profound in care and adoption proceedings in public law, as they can result in siblings being separated with limited or no effective provision for contact.*

and furthermore that:

> *When siblings are not placed together, adoption is the most serious risk to the continuity of their relationship. Three powerful assumptions may outweigh the promotion of anything other than indirect contact: that expectations of direct contact will deter potential adopters; that post-adoption contact should and can only take place with the agreement of adopters; and, that the security and stability of placements will be undermined by contact with siblings living with or in contact with birth relatives.*

Considering the ethical issues in adoption planning for siblings, a report by BASW (Featherstone *et al*, 2018, p27) noted that:

> *There was consensus that there is no one solution that works for all, and it is crucial to attend to particular children's and families' circumstances. In principle, siblings should be placed together, but an individualised and nuanced response is vital. If siblings are separated some form of contact between them should be aimed for, and direct contact should not be rejected simply because one child is living with, or in contact with, the birth family.*

The report stated that the importance of children's sibling relationships was recognised by all groups of respondents. Birth parents wanted their children to be placed together, if possible, and also stressed the importance of acknowledging the needs and views of siblings; some adopted people highlighted that the loss of relationships with brothers and sisters had life-long implications for them and their sense of self:

> *I feel it would be very important for the adoptees to have the rock of where you have come from and it's very important for self-confidence, security, identity and roots. You have a mirror image of where you have come from. It's so important to keep siblings together if both going through adoption.*
>
> (Quoted in Featherstone *et al*, 2018, p26)

and:

> *I will be legally unrelated to my birth sibling for my entire life, and our children will also be unrelated. This is in spite of us always considering ourselves as siblings and acting as such.*
>
> (Quoted in Featherstone *et al*, 2018, p27)

However, research on outcomes in respect of sibling placements is not straightforward. Different definitions have been used, study samples vary (for example, whether or not older children who experienced greater adversity are included), and whilst some associations have been identified, causality is far harder to determine. As Dibben *et al* (2018, p5) recently summarised:

> *Overall, the research in the area of sibling placement is, however, only marginally favourable to sibling placement together. Although it is possible to identify strong research that points in favour of sibling placement together, similarly, it is possible to find research that points against sibling placement.*

Research on outcomes is important but is not the only consideration. Human rights and the need to value children's existing relationships are also significant considerations. There are clearly many challenges but a determined focus on high quality, child-centred services for brothers and sisters has huge potential benefits for large numbers of children. The vast majority of children who are looked after have siblings and typically they come from larger and more complex sibling groups: an average group size of just over four (Kosonen, 1999; Jones and Henderson, 2017) compared with community samples of just over two children. Jones and Henderson also noted that more than two-thirds of looked after children were living apart from at least one of their familiar biological siblings and two-fifths were living apart from all of their familiar biological siblings.

These sibling groups are more likely to include one or more children who share one rather than both parents; they may be of different ethnicity; and the children are highly likely to have some additional needs. The timing of children's entry into care may differ – one or more siblings may become looked after whilst others remain at home or are placed with relatives. When brothers and sisters are placed in different settings, children may deeply grieve the loss of these relationships. Older children may have cared for younger siblings from whom they become separated. They may cherish memories of and for them, which might be accessed by younger brothers and sisters many years later. For others, this opportunity may never arise as life paths diverge and differences become unbridgeable.

There is both evidence and experience that challenge us to better understand and address the impact of early trauma within birth families, some of which can and does impact on relationships between brothers and sisters. Given this context and complexity, it is unsurprising that decisions about placing siblings "together or apart" weigh heavily on those involved. These decisions will be some of the most emotionally demanding and challenging ones that social workers make, so how can we conduct the fairest assessments for all involved? How should we involve children and those who know them best? How do we evidence and explain the decisions that we make? And, if brothers and sisters cannot live together, what contact and knowledge might benefit them, and their carers? These and other key questions are considered and efforts made to explore and address them within this practice guide.

The guide primarily focuses on the needs of brothers and sisters, individually and in groups, for whom a permanent placement seems likely or has already been determined as the plan. However, some of the material is also relevant for managers and practitioners working to provide a service that proactively considers the needs of siblings who become looked after. For example, the importance of effective early planning when siblings enter foster care together, or enter care sequentially in quick succession, is emphasised (see Chapter 3). A central tenet of the guide is that a step-by-step approach from the outset will help promote better outcomes for children both individually and as a sibling group. Initial decisions and planning – particularly whether brothers and sisters are placed together or not – will inevitably affect how relationships are subsequently viewed and assessed by practitioners. For example, there is an inherent risk that the initial placement decisions will be maintained rather than challenged and changed.

Many children entering public care in the UK are separated from one or more of their siblings – typically this happens because there are insufficient foster placements to meet the needs of sibling groups in general and larger groups in particular. The use of residential care to keep brothers and sisters together is now rare. In some instances, brothers and sisters enter care at different times. Others are separated because of abusive or problematic interactions that have already been identified within the family. Hastily-made, pragmatic and resource-driven decisions as to which children are placed together may have a long reach, yet within this context there are still many choices that we can actively make – in particular, the ways in which children living apart are supported to develop or maintain relationships with brothers and sisters placed elsewhere. For example: should overnight sibling contact be expected as accepted good practice in foster care rather than a rarity?

With regard to assessments, there is a strong emphasis in this guide on multi-sourcing information and corroborating evidence wherever possible. The importance of a collaborative approach between families, social workers and foster carers, working together and with others, to understand and nurture children's needs, is core to a high-quality service. The ways in which links and contact are promoted between foster carers and the children for whom they are providing care is one key component that will not only benefit children but also, and crucially so, can inform the assessment process. Similarly, it is evident that parents and relatives hold a deep reservoir of knowledge about

INTRODUCTION

children's sibling relationships. The context of each child's experiences and history, and whether adults have shaped and reinforced patterns of interaction, or valued one child over another, will be crucial to understand. The impact of differential treatment and other factors are explored to help practitioners make plans that are more likely to promote better outcomes for children.

The contributions of other key professionals are emphasised. Health visitors' observations of pre-school children can include helpful information regarding siblings within the family home as well as the impact of early care and parenting factors. Similarly, pre-school and school staff are likely to have a good understanding of young children with whom they work and typically this might include working knowledge of a child's family and sibling relationships. The ways in which we plan assessments and seek out and make use of significant, available sources of knowledge and understanding will impact on the quality and coherence of sibling assessments. Within the appendices to this guide, you can access semi-structured forms and other tools to help frame and inform your own observations. The challenge of analysis and making considered plans is addressed: for example, how do you understand and balance the information and evidence before you?

The experiences of families who adopt intact sibling groups or who care for one or more children are reviewed alongside the voices and experiences of siblings who are adopted. Adoptive parents tell us that they want and need more help with sibling relationships and issues but that this is not readily available. Contact and support services to promote better outcomes for children and families are briefly considered (see Chapter 11).

This guide focuses on children being placed permanently away from their birth families, but has wider applicability. Chapter 2 on sibling relationships will be especially relevant for practitioners working with families where brothers and sisters have experienced adversity. Given the complexities of sibling relationships, the guide encourages all of those working with looked after children to avoid "all or nothing" choices and planning decisions for siblings. Whilst individually we may aim to avoid unnecessary losses for children, in practice this is much more difficult to achieve if policy and service provision do not underpin our work. If children are placed separately in foster care, how do services set out to encompass and try to address children's needs and concerns? What might a truly "sibling-friendly" service look like from the perspective of children? For example, if we focus on what each child might need to know and might need to have, then the following charter for brothers and sisters might become more anchored in practice.

A CHARTER FOR BROTHERS AND SISTERS

In foster care

Information and explanations for separated brothers and sisters in foster care are crucially important. A quality service from the perspective of children might helpfully include the following:

- I know why it wasn't possible to place us together.
- I know where my brothers and sisters are living.
- I know how I can contact my brothers and sisters.
- I know when I will see my brothers and sisters.
- I have photos of my brothers and sisters.
- My social worker has talked to all of us about why we are in foster care.
- I sometimes have/have had life history sessions that include my brothers and sisters.
- My foster carer knows important details about my brothers and sisters.
- I know that I can talk to my foster carer and social worker about my brothers and sisters – including any mixed up, confusing feelings that I might have.
- I know that my foster carer and social worker will help me to maintain links with my brothers and sisters.
- My social worker has written down the dates of my brothers' and sisters' birthdays and given these to me.
- I know that my foster carer knows how to contact the foster carers of my brothers and sisters.
- I know that my social worker thinks carefully about how to help me and my brothers and sisters and wants to make the best plans for all of us.
- I know that my social worker and foster carer will try to help if I have problems or fall-outs with a sibling.
- I know that my social worker works in a department that thinks relationships between brothers and sisters are really important – not just now but for when I'm older.

In permanent placements

In the context of separation by adoption or other permanent placements for one or more children...

- I know the reasons why I am not living with all my brothers and sisters.

- I have information and explanations in my life story book about my brothers and sisters.
- I have met the family who care for my brothers and sisters.
- I know that my family met my brothers and sisters and have photos of us all together.
- I receive news about my brothers and sisters and how they are doing.
- I have recent photos of my brothers and sisters.
- I know when I will see my brothers and sisters (or why I cannot see them).
- I know that I can talk about and ask questions about my brothers and sisters.

Many children who become looked after and require a permanent placement to meet their needs will be young, pre-school-aged children and will have "future needs" for information and explanations to be accessible to them and their family. The importance of planning and addressing these issues requires a life-course perspective, as the decisions that are made will ripple and resonate throughout each child's journey into and throughout adulthood.

CORE VALUES AND PRINCIPLES

This guide asserts that practice should stem from a rights-based and child-centred approach, wherein children's relationships with their brothers and sisters are valued and accorded priority alongside each child's individual needs. We need to listen to and be thoughtful about what children tell us through their words and behaviour. When their views have been sought, children and young people have consistently told us that their sibling relationships are important to them and should be respected. This does not mean that these relationships are always loving and straightforward, nor does it mean that all children can be placed together with their siblings. However, it does mean that:

- sibling relationships always need to be carefully considered; and
- we should be rigorous in making plans that not only recognise the current state of children's sibling relationships but also their capacity for change during childhood and beyond.

HOW TO MAKE BEST USE OF THIS GUIDE

There is a lot of material in this guide that should be of general interest to child care practitioners and managers, whether their focus is on early intervention with families, foster care or adoption. Each chapter covers distinct aspects but also, to varying degrees, builds on what has been set out in earlier sections. Children's journeys from entry into care are followed through to placement for adoption and beyond. Some chapters will be of particular value to practitioners as they embark on specific pieces of work. For example:

- **For social workers who are working with a sibling group that is about to come into care or has recently been placed in foster care**, Chapter 3, *Becoming looked after: placement, contact and early planning for brothers and sisters*, is likely to be most relevant. This chapter encourages a clear focus on taking steps to promote children's needs and their sibling relationships as well as to start to collate information that will be useful – for example, see the various forms provided in Appendix 2. Chapter 2 will also help to provide a good background knowledge of what factors impact on children's relationships with their brothers and sisters.

- **For practitioners who are conducting an assessment of children's sibling relationships and permanent placement options**, Chapter 5, *Assessment: what you should include and why*, will probably be the best place to start, as well as reading Chapter 2. There is a clear focus on multi-sourcing assessments by involving parents, children, carers, contact supervisors, and professionals working in health and education settings (see forms in Appendix 2). Chapter 6 focuses on the importance of involving children and provides a range of resources to support assessment work with them. An understanding of research and placement outcomes, as set out in Chapter 10, will also be important to consider before permanent placement decisions are made.

- **Fostering teams** may find Chapters 2, 3, 5, 7 and 8 especially relevant to their work. Particular attention is drawn to Chapters 3 and 5 in respect of the role of foster carers in supporting and assessing children's sibling relationships, whether this is through a shared foster placement or by providing observations about contact. Chapter 8 focuses on working with foster carers during transition to permanence. The emotional readiness of foster carers to prepare children to move is emphasised, alongside ways in which carers can work well with adoptive parents; experienced foster carers provide their own ideas and tips for successful transitions.

- **Adoption teams** are likely to find much of the above also relevant to their work. In particular, Chapter 2 helps to provide a good background knowledge of what factors impact on children's sibling relationships, and some of this will be useful to share with prospective adopters and adoptive parents at different points in their journey. Having an understanding of what should be included in a comprehensive sibling assessment, as set out in Chapter 5, will clearly be important and sometimes adoption staff may be tasked with undertaking these assessments or advising on them. Chapter 7 will be of particular relevance to staff involved in the recruitment, preparation and assessment of adopters and this chapter also includes both messages from research and ideas to incorporate at different stages. Chapter 8, *Preparing to move, matching and introductions*, encourages a clear focus on the emotional needs of the adults, but most importantly those of the children. Chapter 9 addresses post-placement contact, highlighting research findings, the importance of carefully balancing risks as well as benefits for children, and emphasising support to all parties. Chapter 10, *Research: how children and their families fare*, provides an overview of research on outcomes, whilst Chapter 11 draws this together to focus on *Planning the right support for children and families*.

Chapter 2
Children's sibling relationships: what helps or hinders them?

INTRODUCTION

This chapter considers some of what we know about relationships between brothers and sisters: how relationships develop and what might help and/or hinder how siblings get on. The impact of adversity, including growing up in households marred by violence, is considered. The importance of addressing problematic patterns of behaviour, including aggression between siblings, is highlighted as these difficulties are likely to "spill over" into relationships with others. For example, a child who shows very domineering behaviour towards brothers and sisters at home is likely to show similar patterns towards children in other settings such as nursery and school.

CHILDREN'S RELATIONSHIPS WITH BROTHERS AND SISTERS

Relationships between siblings that start from birth or early childhood often endure into old age, and are usually much longer than relationships with parents, their own children, or partners. How these relationships develop will depend on many things: for example, how might exposure to high levels of conflict, such as repeated episodes of domestic violence, impact on sibling relationships?

Brothers and sisters usually, but not always, share at least one birth parent and will also usually, but not always, have lived in the same family as other children. However, they can often be as different from each other in character and temperament as unrelated individuals. Each family is unique so it will always be important to obtain a good understanding of each child's experience within the family as well as differing perspectives from parents, significant family members and children themselves.

As with all close relationships, sibling relationships hold the potential for considerable change across the lifespan – their meaning, value and quality may increase or diminish in response to the challenges and changes that each individual experiences. Many adults can recall occasions when they were deliberately unkind or even cruel to their siblings as well as times when they felt closer to their brother or sister than to anyone else.

During the first two years of life, children start to develop a range of social–emotional, cognitive and behavioural skills. These core skills will prove crucial in helping to promote relationships with siblings and peers as well as having wider benefits, such as allowing an easier transition to nursery and school. They include:

- sharing adult/parental attention;
- regulating emotions;
- being able to inhibit impulses;
- imitating another child's actions;
- understanding cause-and-effect relationships; and
- developing language skills.

Young children spend more time interacting with their siblings than anyone else, including parents. Interactions between brothers and sisters are characterised by both strong positive features, such as warmth and intimacy, as well as negative qualities, such as intense conflict (Feinberg *et al*, 2012). Sibling relationships can be harmonious (high warmth, low hostility), affectively intense (high warmth and hostility), hostile (low warmth, high hostility), and uninvolved (low warmth and hostility) (McGuire *et al*, 1996). The first three patterns are evident in childhood, but the last is typically apparent only in older adolescents (Buist and Vermande, 2014). Sibling conflict and aggression may be particularly problematic in a relationship also lacking in warmth (Buist and Vermande, 2014).

During early childhood, sibling relationships may be intense, as pre-school children typically spend a lot of time together but have not yet developed the capacity to regulate their emotions. Relationships can be volatile, quickly changing from shared fun to anger and conflict. The intimate environment shared and knowledge gained about their sibling provides each child with rich opportunities to provide support and comfort as well as teasing.

Howe and Recchia (2014) summarised four major characteristics of sibling relationships that are prominent during early childhood:

- Interactions are emotionally charged such that relationships are typically defined by strong, uninhibited emotions of a positive, negative and sometimes ambivalent quality.

- They are defined by intimacy: because young children spend large amounts of time playing together, they know each other very well – they have the power and knowledge to support, to tease and to annoy. 'This long history and intimate knowledge translates into opportunities for providing emotional and instrumental support for one another, engaging in pretend play, for conflict, and for understanding others' points of view' (p17).

- They are characterised by large individual differences in the quality of children's relationships with one another.

- The age difference between children within a sibling group often makes the issues of power and control, as well as rivalry and jealousy, sources of contention for children, but can also provide a context for more pro-social exchanges, such as teaching, helping and caring actions.

Older or more developmentally advanced siblings can informally teach brothers and sisters a great deal, for example, six-year-olds have been observed to engage in just over two teaching interactions per hour with their four-year-old siblings (Howe *et al*, 2015).

The ways in which a child develops an understanding of the needs, wants and personalities of their sibling/s, and is able to tolerate and appreciate these differences, will have an impact on other relationships. In short, if a child has established coercive behaviours towards their siblings, we should not be surprised to see these patterns "spill over" into other relationships, such as with peers in education settings. By the same token, Howe and Recchia (2014) noted that young siblings who engaged in creative and frequent pretend play demonstrated greater understanding of others, and were more able to construct shared meanings and goals in play. Children's social understanding and capacity to manage conflict are not only important within sibling relationships but also have resonance more widely in terms of peer relationships and adjustment to school.

As Selwyn (2018) has pointed out, our understanding of normative sibling relationships is limited: most studies have examined biological sibling pairs growing up in two-parent, white families. Little is known about sibling relationships within larger sibling groups, the development of sibling relationships among different cultures or where siblings have experienced abusive and traumatic early experiences. Similarly, our understanding of children's sibling relationships in foster care and adoptive family life is limited.

Children who are twins, triplets or quads may share an especially close bond and similarities arising from shared genetic and environmental influences. There is relatively little research that has focused on twin relationships as a distinct type of sibling relationship. Fortuna *et al* (2010) noted that relationships between twins have been depicted as closer and more co-dependent than non-twin siblings. Siblings who are closest in age tend to have higher ratings of rivalry than twins. Fortuna *et al* (p211) noted that:

> ....variables other than genetic similarity appear to play a role in differentiating twins from other siblings, lending support for the idea that there is something unique about the bond between twins, who go through development together, which promotes greater closeness, reliance, and acceptance of the other's needs, including those that conflict with one's own.

These ratings of twins' relationships were based on mothers' accounts and may partly, at least, reflect maternal perceptions about twins sharing a special bond.

Segal (2012) has also studied twins extensively. The Landmark Minnesota Twin Study provided evidence of the genetic influence on individual differences in traits such as personality and intelligence.

THE IMPACT OF EARLY FAMILY LIFE, PARENTING, EMOTIONAL WARMTH AND DIFFERENTIAL TREATMENT

Children entering care and subsequently requiring a permanent placement outside their birth family will typically have experienced multiple adversities. Understanding the impact of the type of parenting and any adversity that children have experienced is central to the assessments that social workers will routinely undertake. There are huge individual differences in response to early experiences, and children's lived experience and perceptions may also differ – that is, not all children in a family will "see" or "feel" things in the same way. Consequently, it will always be important to focus on an individual child and their specific history, experience and response.

Children may experience a range of adversities that not only affect their individual development but may also impact on their relationships with others. Each child's experience of family life may also be shaped by factors such as their position in the family; their sex, ethnicity and culture (if different from that of their siblings); and their capabilities and personality. However, structural variables such as birth order are now generally understood to be less important than qualitative aspects such as the emotional climate within the home: for example, is family life relatively calm or riven by conflict?

Pike *et al* (2009) found that factors, such as whether or not home life was structured and organised, felt safe, focused on each child's needs, and whether each parent showed appropriate affection and involvement, explained the quality of sibling relationships more than "structural" variables such as children's age, sex or intelligence. As Pike *et al* (2009) noted:

> *Enhancing sibling relationships has very little to do with family structure, age spacing, or even the sex constellation of sibling pairs. Instead, our findings indicate that children's individual characters and the family environment are important factors in determining whether brothers and sisters become friends or foes.*

Children are more likely to report greater closeness when they grow up in families with better and more open communication (Samek and Rueter, 2011). Engaging in some structured activities also seems to help nurture relationships between brothers and sisters. Tucker *et al* (2008) reported that adolescent siblings who participated in constructive/structured activities – such as playing sports together or having shared hobbies – reported more positive adjustment.

The way in which a child is viewed and treated within the family will also have an effect. A child may have been treated differently by one or both parents. The wider family network may also reinforce victimisation of one child or, by contrast, provide some counter-balance. Even when children are treated equitably, a child may have perceived some outwardly similar experiences within the family home in a different way to brothers or sisters. Sibling relationships and feelings for each other in childhood and over the ensuing years will probably have included a mixture of love, hate, jealousy, rivalry, like and dislike, and there will almost certainly have been episodes of intense conflict as well as ones of shared enjoyment and support. In households where there are more than two siblings, there are likely to be changes in paired allegiances over the years.

Differential parental treatment has been linked to more sibling conflict, antagonism, and coercive patterns of behaviour. Children tend to consider differential affection as more unfair than differential treatment in general. It seems that children may be more able to tolerate "unequal" rules and chores on the basis of age difference than to cope with differences in affection shown to them. Children are more likely to develop behavioural problems if they perceive differential treatment as being unfair.

Buist *et al* (2013) conducted a meta-analysis (a statistical analysis that combines results) of 34 studies. They investigated the link between child and adolescent sibling relationship quality, looking at warmth, conflict and differential treatment, to examine the impact of these aspects on internalising and externalising problems. They found that children and adolescents who have warmer and less conflictual sibling relationships show significantly fewer problem behaviours, as do children and adolescents who experience less differential treatment by parents. **The finding that sibling conflict has a stronger impact than sibling warmth is noteworthy.** Although emotional warmth and conflict co-occur in most sibling relationships, it seems especially important to focus interventions on decreasing conflicts between brothers and sisters. Other relevant findings were that:

- boys seemed slightly more sensitive to differential treatment in comparison to their brother than girls in comparison to their sister, and responded to this inequality with increases in anxiety and depression;

- siblings closer in age may experience conflicts more intensely – this was linked to stronger feelings of anxiety and depression;

- the impact of differential treatment was more marked for children than for adolescents. Adolescents' increased focus on peers may make them less aware of differential treatment and thus less susceptible to its impact.

The authors noted the limitations of their study (p103), including that it was based on correlational data, so causal interpretations should not be made. They noted that:

> *The influence pattern may well be bi-directional: child and adolescent psychopathology may also affect sibling relationship quality. For example, parents may begin to show more affection towards a well-behaved child as a response to aggressive behaviour of his or her sibling, or sibling relationships may become less warm and more conflictive as a result of child withdrawal or delinquency.*

In a study of adoption disruption, Selwyn *et al* (2014, p28) highlighted that it was important to identify aggressive behaviour of young children in foster care and intervene to address this, as research in general population samples highlights that most children will not "grow out of it". Selwyn *et al* (p15) also cited research on factors that increased the risk of child aggression, such as exposure to domestic violence, paternal behaviours, neglect when under the age of two, and exposure to alcohol *in utero*.

ADVERSE CHILDHOOD EXPERIENCES AND SIBLING RELATIONSHIPS

The ACE (Adverse Childhood Experiences) Study (Centers for Disease Control and Prevention *et al*, 2014) has shown how adverse childhood experiences are strongly related to various risk factors, including for disease throughout the lifespan. The study considered the impact of 10 adverse childhood experiences:

- physical abuse;
- sexual abuse;
- emotional abuse;
- physical neglect;
- emotional neglect;
- mother treated violently;
- household substance abuse;
- household mental illness;
- parental separation or divorce;
- household member in prison.

Most children who are placed for adoption have been exposed to multiple ACEs, with recent research showing that exposure to four or more ACEs is common (see Meakings *et al*, 2017b, 2018; see also Chapter 10).

THE IMPACT OF DOMESTIC VIOLENCE, FEAR AND UNCERTAINTY

The National Scientific Council on the Developing Child aims to translate complex research about early brain development to make it useful to practitioners and decision-makers. A range of helpful publications is available on its website, including a report on the impact of persistent fear and anxiety. This report (2010, p5) highlighted that:

Children raised in physically abusive households show heightened sensitivity (compared with non-abused children) to angry faces, which negatively affects their brain function and behaviour. Learning to identify anger – quickly and successfully – in order to avoid being harmed is a highly adaptive and appropriate response to an abusive environment. However, an increased tendency to assume someone is angry when his or her facial expression is ambiguous can be inappropriate and maladaptive in a typical, non-threatening social setting and even dangerous in unfamiliar social settings.

And:

Children who have had chronic and intensely fearful experiences may lose the capacity to differentiate between threat and safety. This impairs their ability to learn and interact with others, because they frequently perceive threat in familiar social circumstances, such as in the playground or in school. These responses inhibit their ability to learn and often lead to serious anxiety disorders. Young children who have been exposed to traumatic circumstances also have difficulty identifying and responding to different expressions of emotions, and, therefore, have trouble forming healthy relationships. These deficits lead to general problems with social interaction, such as understanding others' facial expressions and emotions.

Findings have generally been consistent with regard to what has been termed a "spillover process", such that hostility and conflict between parents and negativity in parent–child relationships are linked to increased sibling conflict. However, research has also shown that some children and young people show "compensatory" behaviours, forming closer relationships that help to protect them from adjustment problems. As McHale *et al* (2012) set out, an important step is to identify the conditions under which spillover versus compensatory processes emerge. Whilst this research is at an early stage, it is important to recognise that there can be differing impacts on children exposed to similar adversity. **Individual assessment will always be both important and necessary.**

Most of the available research that has considered the impact and consequences of domestic violence has focused on violence between adults, and more specifically violence directed by men towards women and mothers. Teicher and Vitaliano (2011) identified that the potential consequences of witnessing violence to siblings had been almost entirely overlooked. They conducted an important piece of research that found that subjects reported witnessing violence to their siblings slightly more often than witnessing violence to their mothers (22% versus 21%), and that witnessing both forms overlapped by 51–54 per cent. Witnessing violence towards siblings was associated with significant effects on all ratings.

Measures of the relative importance of witnessing violence to siblings were considerably greater (that is, associated with much greater effects on psychiatric symptom ratings) than measures of the importance of witnessing violence towards mothers or fathers. The effects of witnessing violence towards the latter were predominantly indirect and mediated by changes in maternal behaviour. The effects of witnessing violence towards siblings were more direct. These findings suggest that more attention should be given to the effects of witnessing aggression toward siblings.

Teicher and Vitaliano (2011) postulated that children who witnessed violence towards siblings, but were largely spared themselves, may suffer from "survivor's guilt". Guilt may be compounded when a child had tended to side with the abusive parent and shared in their brother or sister's maltreatment. Importantly, and as others have done, the authors noted the possible impact of living in a home where fear and uncertainty are pervasive; this may be more stressful then experiencing physical abuse directly.

BULLYING AND PEER AND SIBLING RELATIONSHIPS

The link between bullying of peers and sibling bullying is crucially important to understand and has implications for early intervention as well as placement planning. Children who are exposed to negative parenting – including abuse, neglect but also overprotection – are more likely to experience childhood bullying by their peers. A meta-analysis of 70 studies of more than 200,000 children (Lereya et al, 2013) also found that the effects of poor parenting were stronger for children who were both a victim and perpetrator of bullying (bully-victims) than children who were solely victims. They highlighted the following:

- All children engage in conflict, and this is not a bad thing if it stays within boundaries because it teaches them how to negotiate.

- Home is the place where bullying often begins: it starts between siblings. If a child bullies their brother or sister, they are three times more likely to also bully other children at school. This is learned behaviour.

- In cases where children have had harsh experiences with abusive parents, they are more likely to become a bully-victim or a victim.

- Children with very over-protective parents (so-called helicopter parenting) are more likely to become a pure victim because they never learned how to deal with conflicts.

- Bullies who enter a new classroom will not know beforehand who will become their victim. They will test out their impact on a child, honing in on those who do not just walk away but who are shaken, who may begin to cry. Bullies scan whether these children have friends to help them; if not, they are easy targets where no fights are to be expected. So the individual characteristics of children are important factors in who becomes victimised.

- Psychological characteristics are especially important, such as being vulnerable or emotional or having poor social skills. Physical characteristics matter much less than is often thought.

Social and emotional skills are central to our well-being and fitting in with other children is a crucial life task. How children get on with other children will sow the seeds for future relationships – parents will ultimately die and, in the absence of some supportive relationships, individuals may experience chronic loneliness and isolation.

There is now a growing body of evidence that bullying can have a very serious impact on children's well-being and lead or contribute to a range of adverse outcomes. Sibling bullying increases the risk of being involved in peer bullying, and is independently associated with concurrent and early adult emotional problems, including distress, depression and self-harm. The effects are cumulative, such that children who are bullied by both siblings and peers experience increased emotional problems compared with those bullied by siblings or peers alone (Wolke *et al*, 2015).

A post-placement study by Saunders and Selwyn of sibling groups comprising three or more children highlighted that poor relationships with peers was described as the main area of difficulty. In respect of the children's sibling relationships, the authors noted (2010, p10):

About half the children quarrelled constantly, usually just low level bickering, but four families were concerned that quarrels often turned into physical fights. However, the children were also very close to each other and most spent a lot of time together. The adopters had most difficulty in managing children's challenging behaviours and attachment difficulties, persuading "parentified" children to relinquish the care of their siblings, and meeting the needs of individual children within the sibling group.

Overall, most children in this study were making good progress; many were described as "blossoming", and some of their more severe behaviours had stopped or were diminishing. The majority of adopters felt positively about the decision to keep the siblings together and almost two-thirds of the adopters stated that they would recommend adopting a sibling group.

CAREGIVING BEHAVIOURS

It is important to understand the context in which caregiving behaviour has developed. In some cultures, sibling caregiving may be accepted practice. Caring actions by an older sibling may nurture a sense of esteem for the young carer, who may perceive themselves as performing a vital and valued role within the family. It can promote a sense of interdependence (rather than autonomy), which is valued in many non-Western cultures.

Children's own views, as caregivers and as cared-for, are important. Children may view this very differently to adults. Sibling caregiving was found to be a common experience for school-aged children and was viewed primarily positively both by the caregiver and care-receiver children (Kosonen, 1996). It will always be important to consider behaviour in context and take account of what meaning it may have for children.

DISABILITY

The impact of having a disabled brother or sister needs to be understood in context. For some children, sibling relationships may be close and supportive, whilst for others emotions may be more fraught. It will be important to understand how the disabled child and their particular disability have been perceived by parents and wider family and what the impact is. What is expected of the child's siblings and how have they responded to this? They may be protective of their disabled sibling or may resent their perceived impact on family life. They may experience periods of acceptance as well as periods of resentment and embarrassment – depending on their age and understanding as well as on the attitudes of others, including peers.

Research evidence (Hasting, 2013) indicates that brothers and sisters of children and young people with intellectual and developmental disability overall have a slightly increased risk for problems with well-being and educational attainment. Siblings who are likely to have the most problems are sibling young carers and siblings whose brothers and sisters have behavioural problems. (See also www.sibs.org.uk.)

LINKS BETWEEN FRIENDSHIPS AND SIBLING RELATIONSHIPS

Learning how to make and keep friends is one of the most important challenges of childhood.

(Centre of Excellence for Children's Well-Being, 2009, p1)

The particular challenges that may be faced by looked after children in developing peer relationships has received little attention. Children may experience a fracturing of friendships when they move away from their birth family. Arguably, many children may not have learned the skills for emotional reciprocity and carers as well as adopters report that this is a significant difficulty for children. When conflict and rivalry are problematic features within a child's relationships with brothers and sisters, research tells us that similar issues may be apparent in forming and sustaining friendships.

- Relationships with brothers and sisters play an important part in children's social development. Children with siblings have many opportunities to practise social skills in an intimate and (usually) safe environment.

- Relationships with siblings tend to be emotionally charged. Spending time with their brothers and sisters helps children to learn to deal with strong emotions (positive and negative). They also learn to understand what others think, want and feel, which in turn helps children to learn how to resolve conflicts.

- Young children who learn to co-operate and play well with one another tend to make friends more easily throughout their lives.

- Friendships provide children with valuable learning experiences. When children interact and play with others, they learn the importance of social life and how to control their emotions. These skills are important throughout life.

- Children's social skills make a big difference to whether they are accepted by others or not. The key skills here are:
  - communication: to say what they want and feel, ask questions, invite other children to play;
  - ability to control emotions: to recognise their own emotions and those of others, to control emotional outbursts, and to deal with frustrations;
  - ability to resolve conflicts: to control the impulse to be aggressive, to be able to suggest alternative solutions, and to compromise;
  - co-operation: to take turns, imitate others, react positively to others, and to see others' points of view.

(Adapted from Centre of Excellence for Children's Well-Being, 2009)

Similarly, Tremblay *et al* (2014) state that sibling relationships might be viewed as a special kind of peer relationship that provides an important context for the development of children's understanding of others' worlds, emotions, thoughts, intentions and beliefs. They also note that frequent sibling conflicts during childhood are associated with poor adjustment later in life.

RESEARCH – IMPROVING SIBLING RELATIONSHIPS

When children have experienced early adversity, such as poor parenting, they may not have learned core social–emotional skills during preschool years. This "gap" in their development is likely to make it harder for them to get on well with brothers and sisters, but is also likely to impact adversely on relationships with peers.

A few research studies have evaluated interventions that can help improve sibling relationships (Linares *et al*, 2015; Kothari *et al*, 2017; Waid and Wojciak, 2017). These have generally focused on reducing conflict and aggression, for example, by teaching/coaching parents to become effective mediators. The studies offer an optimistic view, in that changes within sibling relationships can be facilitated through specific interventions, and arguably should serve as an impetus for service development.

KEY POINTS

- Sibling relationships are influenced within the family and by parenting behaviour. The climate of the home, such as whether it feels organised; whether parents show affection; how involved fathers are; and similar factors help explain how siblings get on, better than "structural" variables such as children's age, sex or intelligence.

- Young children spend more time interacting with their siblings than anyone else, including parents, and from a very young age children attend to the ways in which their parents treat them relative to their siblings.

- Sibling relationships provide a context for learning about "how other people tick" and how conflicts are resolved, which may be carried through into other relationships.

- Sibling relationships are often very ambivalent, rapidly switching between warmth and conflict during observed interactions. For example, high warmth may co-exist with high conflict between children. High conflict and low levels of emotional warmth are more worrying. Greater sibling warmth is associated with better individual adjustment. Sibling relationships tend to be more tolerant of conflict than those with peers. Siblings closer in age may experience conflicts more intensely and be more adversely affected.

- Better-quality parental relationships appear to "spill over" into more positive relationships between their children, suggesting that children may learn positive relationship skills from their parents, or that "happy-together" partners are better able to structure their children's environment and respond in ways that help promote better relationships between their children.

- Hostility and conflict between parents and negativity in parent–child relationships are linked to sibling conflict ("spillover" effect). However, research has also shown that some children and young people show "compensatory" behaviours, forming closer relationships that help to protect them from adjustment problems.

- Differential treatment by a parent has been linked to greater sibling conflict. Children are particularly affected by differential affection that is harder for them to perceive as "fair" (as compared to being tasked to do more jobs in the home). Boys may be more sensitive to differential treatment than girls.

- Witnessing violence towards a sibling merits greater attention – it is not only deeply distressing but has a significant impact on brothers and sisters.

- More emotionally volatile children generally have poorer relationships with their siblings. Research found that this was also the case for children who exhibited problem behaviour and poor social competence.

- Poor sibling relationships can contribute to the development of peer aggression, bullying and rejection by peers. Home is the place where bullying often begins. If a child bullies their brother or sister, they are three times more likely to also bully other children at school. This is learned behaviour.

- Interventions designed to reduce sibling conflicts and increase pro-social behaviours are promising and can help prevent difficulties in relationships.

Practice point

When a child is separated from siblings because of concerns about their behaviour, issues relating to aspects such as managing emotions and differences still need to be addressed. Reparative work that focuses on the sibling relationship is part of the foster carer's role. Foster carers, and the children whom they care for, may need access to specialist services to help reduce conflicts between children and promote positive behaviour. In the absence of such support, difficulties may well impact on other relationships, such as those with peers.

Chapter 3
Becoming looked after: early planning, placement and contact for brothers and sisters

INTRODUCTION

This chapter focuses on the importance of early, proactive placement planning and considers what will help children if they have to be placed apart and what they themselves tell us about how much their relationships with brothers and sisters matter. Research on foster placement outcomes in respect of siblings is also briefly reviewed.

There is an emphasis on the steps that can be taken that will helpfully contribute to a balanced and child-centred assessment of children and their sibling relationships, for example:

- ensuring that observations of the children during parental contact/family time* include consideration of how siblings interact with one another as well as parental behaviour towards each child. This, together with other actions, can help you identify and/or evidence patterns of behaviour such as differential treatment by parents (see Appendix 2 for forms to use);

- ensuring that children's foster carers work constructively with you, so that their observations about and relationships with the children can effectively inform the assessment process as it evolves;

- drawing on the knowledge and experience of health and education professionals that focuses on sibling relationships (see Appendix 2 for form and tools to use);

---

* The term "contact" is often used in this publication and in research or guidance that is referred to; however, it is recognised that in discussions with children and family members, the use of language such as "visits" "family time" or "seeing your brothers and sisters" is more appropriate.

- undertaking an SDQ (Strengths and Difficulties Questionnaire, (Goodman, 1997)) assessment early on with foster carers and education staff for all children aged three years and above.

CHILDREN AND YOUNG PEOPLE – WHAT MATTERS TO THEM

Listening to children and young people's wishes and feelings should be universal, but it isn't.

How children feel about their lives and the care they receive should be central to understanding the quality of care, but it isn't.

Instead it is often adults – carers and professionals – who share their own interpretations of how a positive care system does and should look. There is an urgent need for local authorities and national decision-makers to understand how their services impact on the children they support and how well the needs of children are being met, to ensure those services are responsive to children's views and needs.

(Selwyn and Briheim-Crookall, 2017)

Children and young people generally tell us that they want to be placed together with their brothers and sisters, but if this does not or cannot happen, they want their social workers to help them to keep in touch. For example, Morgan (2009) found that most children in care thought it important to keep siblings together whilst three-quarters thought that they should be helped to keep in touch with their brothers and sisters if they had to live apart. One young person said that social workers should:

Try their hardest to keep them together but if they don't, make sure they don't drift apart and become more like distant relatives than brothers and sisters.

A review of existing research (Hadley Centre and Coram Voice, 2015) on young people's views of their care experiences identified the following:

- Maintaining and developing warm, trusting relationships with adults, friends and family members was of "over-riding importance", yet many studies reported that young people thought that these relationships were not prioritised.

- Sibling contact or keeping siblings together in the same placement was important for children.

- Some young people described feeling a sense of support from their siblings, as they were the only ones who could truly understand what they were experiencing.

- Separation from siblings was particularly devastating when those children and young people had previously been responsible for caring for other – typically younger – siblings.

At the same time, children and young people were realistic in recognising that it was not always possible to place siblings together, but if separation had to happen, then:

- more effort needed to be put into promoting contact between siblings; and
- they needed to feel involved and to know why certain plans had been made.

RESEARCH – PLACEMENT TOGETHER IN FOSTER CARE

Research on placement outcomes for children placed together or apart from siblings is complex and, unsurprisingly, does not provide a single solution that applies to all children. Placement outcomes are affected by numerous variables. Outcomes are influenced by factors relating to each child, the adopters or other long-term carers, and agency practice such as preparation and support. The complexity of children's pre-placement experiences will clearly have an impact but is not deterministic; outcome research is based on populations and probabilities. Research samples may vary widely reflecting the population studied: some may focus on young children who experienced less adversity, whereas others may predominantly focus on older children with more difficult histories.

Children may have always lived together or spent significant time apart – this, combined with the reasons for separation, may impact on children's relationships and outcomes. Leathers (2005) highlighted that children's history of placement together or apart has not been consistently coded across research and that children may be:

- placed alone (and this has always been the case);
- placed alone (with a history of sibling placement);
- placed with sibling/s (with a history of inconsistency);
- placed with sibling/s (and has always been placed with sibling/s).

A review of research studies identified considerable variability in approach and also stressed that causality and relationships between the many variables were complex:

The direction of the relationship between variables cannot be inferred or assumed from all the studies in this review. Whilst it may be shown, for example, that children in placement with siblings have fewer emotional and behavioural difficulties than those separated from their siblings,

> *it is not known whether higher levels of emotional and behavioural difficulties led to a greater likelihood of being placed separately, or whether being placed separately led to a decline in emotional and behavioural well-being.*
>
> (Meakings *et al*, 2017b, p10)

A large study of foster placement disruptions in Texas considered the reason placements ended and age-specific risk factors associated with placement instability. Placements of all siblings together led to a lower risk of disruptions due to incompatibility between the child and caregiver or child-initiated disruptions (e.g. the child ran away or refused to stay) compared with placements of siblings placed apart (Sattler *et al*, 2018). This finding supported the authors' hypothesis that this may reflect siblings' motivation to stay together. However, placement with all siblings increased some other types of instability (specifically of a substandard care disruption).

We are starting to understand more about the ways in which relationships between brothers and sisters can promote placement stability as well as supporting emotional and relational well-being. However, research findings and their limitations also need to be borne in mind. Benefits that have been identified for placing siblings together include:

- increased chances of achieving reunification, and some limited findings suggest more favourable educational outcomes than for siblings living separately (Meakings *et al*, 2017);

- easing the transition into care because there is continuity of family relationships (Herrick and Piccus, 2005; Leathers, 2005). In an unknown, unfamiliar situation, the presence of one or more siblings can play a crucial role in maintaining emotional stability and a sense of safety (Shlonsky *et al*, 2005);

- better emotional support: care-experienced young people typically report that being placed with siblings was experienced by them as being emotionally supportive, helping to provide them with a ready-made support group, an ally, someone to talk to if they had problems, and someone on whom they could depend;

- warm sibling relationships that can help protect the emotional well-being of children and young people in care (Wojciak *et al*, 2013);

- particular benefits for boys, helping them to develop relationship skills and competence, perhaps because boys may otherwise have fewer opportunities outside their sibling relationships to develop these qualities (Richardson and Yates, 2014).

For many siblings, placement together will clearly be the preferred and right choice. For some children, their relationships with brothers and sisters will suggest or require different placement plans. For others, a lack of suitable placements will lead to children being placed separately. Work may need to be planned with children to minimise the impact of separation. Whether children are placed together or apart, work will often need to be done to better understand and help repair their relationships.

EARLY PLANNING AND PLACING CHILDREN

Local authorities should place a child with siblings where practicable and provided that it is in the best interests of each child. (s.22c, Children Act 1989)

As noted in the Introduction, hastily-made, pragmatic and resource-driven decisions as to which children are placed together will have a long-term impact. It can be hard to change or to challenge early placement plans and decisions with the risk that these continue through to the permanency plan. This chapter focuses on early planning issues and considers what can help, regardless of whether or not brothers and sisters can all be placed in the same foster home. There are many choices that we can actively make – in particular, the ways in which separated siblings are supported to develop and maintain relationships with their brothers and sisters.

The Care Inquiry (2013) highlighted that:

Given that sibling relationships are likely to be among the most long lasting and significant relationships in a child's life, siblings should be placed together unless there are strong evidence-based reasons for not doing so. In any such case, the future significance of these sibling relationships and their potential positive benefit should be recognised and actively developed.

(2013, para 5.6)

The Department for Education (2018a, p9) set out key elements of a well functioning foster care system based on two reviews and the evidence underpinning them. The five overarching ambitions are:

- *Children are listened to and involved in decisions about their lives.*
- *Foster carers receive the support and respect they need and deserve to care for children.*
- *There are enough high-quality fostering placements, in the right place, at the right time.*
- *Local authorities commission placements according to the needs of the child.*

- *Children experience stability regardless of the permanence plan.*

It is important that policy and service provision specifically focus on the needs of sibling groups – brothers and sisters represent a significant need that merits targeted attention. Children who are looked after are more likely to have brothers and sisters than the general population and to have more of them. In about four-fifths of cases, social workers assess that siblings needed to be placed together in foster care (Ofsted, 2015). However, studies show that some factors increase the risk of separation (Hegar, 2005; Meakings *et al*, 2017a):

- a larger sibling group;
- the children are older;
- a larger age gap between siblings;
- entering care at different times;
- one or more children have special needs;
- children have not been placed with kinship carers;
- placement changes have been more frequent and recent.

Importantly, Meakings *et al* (2017a) also highlighted that brothers and sisters placed together at the outset were more likely to remain together over time, whilst those who had been separated at the outset were more likely to remain apart.

It is clear, then, that the priority accorded to planning for sibling groups will impact on a range of connected issues, for example, whether or not a local authority targets sibling carer recruitment and addresses associated support needs. Action for Children found that about one-third of the children from sibling groups who were placed in foster care between April 2013 and March 2014 were separated from their siblings. The survey revealed considerable variation between authorities (from 19 per cent separation up to 45 per cent). More than half of the children who had been split from their siblings said it made them feel 'upset and angry'. Sir Tony Hawkhead, Chief Executive of Action for Children, said in a press release at the time:

> *Splitting siblings can ignite feelings of loss and abandonment which can affect emotional and mental health. They increase the risk of unstable foster placements and poor performance at school, as well as further problems in adulthood, such as difficulty finding a job, drug and alcohol addiction, homelessness or criminal activity...We know that in some cases children can be so badly hurt by what has happened to them before going into care, including severe neglect and abuse, that they need one-to-one support. In the vast majority of cases, however, siblings benefit hugely by staying together and that's why we need more foster carers to help them.*

More recently, a BBC Freedom of Information request sent to more than 200 UK local authorities revealed that more than half of sibling groups in care are split up, with more than 12,000 children not living with at least one of their siblings (Kenyon and Forde, 2020). Figures also showed that at least 1,375 children who were placed for adoption between April 2018 and November 2019 had been separated from birth siblings. However, the actual figures could be higher because one-third of local authorities did not provide data.

FOSTER FAMILIES

There is a critical shortage of foster carers throughout the UK and this results in large numbers of children becoming separated on entry into care. As discussed earlier (see Chapter 2), this can have distressing and long-term consequences, leading, as it may do, to the permanent separation of brothers and sisters, and in other cases, making a joint permanent placement much harder to achieve.

A press release by The Fostering Network (11 May 2017) reported on a survey that it had conducted that found that more than 7,000 new foster families were needed in the next year to ensure that the right placements were available. The survey highlighted that the main areas of need were for families to offer homes to teenagers and groups of brothers and sisters: 86 per cent of fostering services had a particular need for foster carers for sibling groups in England alone. There were 455 groups of siblings who had been separated despite being assessed to live together.

Local authorities have a statutory responsibility under the Sufficiency Duty (see Appendix 1) to ensure that a range of placements through a number of providers is available to meet the local demand and needs of their population of looked after children. Local authorities must be able to show that they are taking strategic steps to meet the sufficiency duty, so far as is "reasonably practicable". Mechanisms should be in place to ensure that professionals involved in placement decisions have sufficient knowledge and information about the supply and quality of placements. When placing a child, the overriding factor is that the placement must be the most appropriate available. Preference must be given to a placement with a friend, relative or other person connected with the child where that is appropriate. Failing that, a placement must be found, so far as is reasonably practicable in all circumstances, that:

- is near the child's home;
- does not disrupt the child's education (or training);
- enables the child to live with an accommodated sibling;

- where the child is disabled, is suitable to meet the needs of that child; and

- is within the local authority's area, unless that is not reasonably practicable.

All of these factors have to be taken into account and are not listed in order of priority. Not being able to place siblings together when this is in their best interests is something that needs to be considered and addressed within recruitment. Equally, there are likely to be approved foster carers who, with additional support or finance to extend or change their home, would be able to accommodate brothers and sisters (Department for Children, Schools and Families, 2010).

Preparing and making best use of foster families

During preparation and in training, it is helpful to think about which elements specifically focus on siblings and aspects that might be led by a care-experienced young person or adult who can talk directly about the impact on them. Sharing the experience of what it was like to be separated from brothers and sisters, or conversely the benefits gleaned from being together, can promote greater understanding. Film material can also be powerful in helping to inform and shape attitudes. Examples might include this, from the *Early Intervention Foundation (EIF)* (19 May 2017):

> *Kerry Littleford shares her moving personal story of growing up in a family wrestling with poverty and the care system. She is then joined in conversation by social affairs journalist Louise Tickle, to discuss the lessons she has learned as an adult and a public health worker, and the difference that early intervention could have made to the lives of her mother and siblings, and to her own childhood experiences.*
>
> (From the EIF National Conference, 11 May 2017, Royal College of Physicians, London)

If families are able to take sibling groups of three or more, single children should not be placed with them if at all possible, although it is acknowledged that this may be very difficult when resources are stretched. From the family's point of view, perhaps a retainer fee could be paid if there is a wait for a sibling group placement.

As with families offering permanence, additional support and practical help will almost certainly be needed when families are caring for three or more children. It is important that carers are aware of what can be provided and that practical aspects do not deter them from looking after siblings. The availability of interventions to address challenging behaviours and difficult interactions within sibling groups will also be central to supporting foster families and the children whom they look after. For example, what specialist input is available to address high levels of conflict between siblings?

As has been discussed earlier, foster carers have a very important role in assessing the attachments and relationships between siblings and in listening to what the individual children in their care say about their brothers and sisters and what they would like for their future. Foster carers and the children's social worker/s need to work closely together, both to facilitate the assessment and to promote contact between siblings who are placed separately. These are all skilled tasks for which thorough preparation as well as good support will be needed. The sections on early planning and assessment in Chapter 3 include key elements and forms (see also Appendix 2) that may helpfully be used when preparing foster carers. Sequential case study material that "follows" a sibling group as they enter care and through to moving on to permanence might helpfully be used across several preparation meetings. For example, a case study that identifies key events and their emotional impact on each individual child might incorporate: the impact of separation on entry into care; planning of contact between foster carers looking after the children; assessment issues; permanency planning; foster carers' role in adoption introductions when children might be reunited or separated; carers supporting an older child whose younger siblings are placed for adoption; and foster carers' involvement in after adoption contact.

Foster carers caring for siblings placed together

Foster carers may require additional practical and emotional support in order to be able to care for a group of brothers and sisters. Additional needs may be apparent from the outset or emerge during the placement. In some cases, the children and their relationships with one another may be well understood and in other cases, very little will be known about how they interact. Separation from parents may be experienced and felt very differently by the children depending on their age, the quality of the care that they received, and other factors. Children may have adopted roles within the family home that are known or have not yet been identified. Children may cling on to or more readily relinquish roles depending on whether certain patterns of behaviour were reinforced and perhaps bolstered their fragile sense of self-esteem, for example, an older child may have felt valued and experienced emotional rewards when comforting a younger sibling. The ways in which foster carers both understand and respond to children's behaviours may be perceived as reassuring or threatening by one or more siblings.

Careful consideration will need to be given to whether or not children share a bedroom. When siblings have been used to sharing a bedroom they may want this to continue, or may welcome having their own bedroom if this is possible. Younger children may have been used to falling asleep downstairs or going to bed at the same time as much older siblings. One or more children may dominate others. Brothers may feel superior to sisters and try to reinforce similar behaviour and expectations within the foster home. Established patterns of behaviour are not easily or quickly changed. Foster carers may have considerable experience managing complex behaviours in respect of individual children, but may struggle when presented with entrenched patterns of interaction between siblings. Particular difficulties can arise when children "gang up" or ally with one another to challenge the carer and their authority.

Foster carers should be asked to provide observations about the children's sibling relationships as well as each child's individual needs and behaviour (see Appendix 2).

Foster carers caring for sibling groups may need additional support over and above that provided by their supervising worker and the children's social worker. Carers and their support workers should be aware of what specialist advice and support can be accessed. For example, psychological intervention may be required to manage behavioural difficulties such as high levels of rivalry and conflict between siblings.

Obtaining a good understanding of each child's behaviour and needs is clearly important. Foster carers should be asked to complete an SDQ for children aged two years and above. High SDQ scores may flag the need for intervention and highlight areas in which one or more of the children is particularly struggling (see Chapter 5).

Foster carers caring for siblings with conflictual and complex relationships

All siblings have some fall-outs and for most children there is underlying warmth for one another such that they quickly make up. When conflict is frequent and there is little emotional warmth, brothers and sisters may experience shared placement as unhelpful and undermining. Chapter 2 notes that some children have very troubled relationships with their siblings and that these may, in part at least, stem from their early experiences and treatment by parents. Chapter 5 (on assessment) also addresses these issues in the context of assessing children's sibling relationships prior to making plans for permanent placement. Foster carers will clearly have important observations to share in respect of children's sibling relationships when they are caring for all of the siblings or for one or more children. They may observe occasional disputes between placed children that they consider to be within normal parameters, or they may be concerned by a high and sustained pattern of conflict between siblings.

In a study of adoption disruptions, Selwyn *et al* (2014, p28) cited studies that had examined factors that increased the risk of child aggression, such as exposure to domestic violence, paternal behaviours, neglect under the age of two, and exposure to alcohol *in utero*. The authors highlighted that it was important to:

> *Identify young children who are aggressive in foster care and intervene to address the aggression. The message from research on aggression in general population samples is that most children will not "grow out of it".*

Physical aggression that is instigated by one child towards other siblings is linked with more adoption difficulties and breakdowns (see Chapter 10). Assessment forms for use with foster carers, included in Appendix 2, encourage clear reporting of strengths and difficulties within the sibling group.

Siblings may be placed apart either because of concerns about their relationships or because there was not a foster home available to keep them together. When children are living apart, the type of contact and frequency of contact that is right for each child will need to be planned, taking into account a range of factors; crucially, this will include the nature of their relationship and children's ascertainable wishes and feelings.

Selwyn (2018, p17) found that a significant proportion of children aged 8–10 felt that they were having too much contact with siblings. The reasons for this were not clear, but the author wondered if sibling conflict was implicated. Some children wrote that they felt their parents treated them differently to their siblings, either during contact or because their brothers and sisters were still living at home. Selwyn cited research on child development by Feinberg *et al* (2012) that identifies parental differential treatment as being associated with greater conflict among siblings and, for the less favoured child, poorer adjustment.

Key practice point

If children express dislike, fear or wariness about a sibling placed with them or with whom they are having contact, then the reasons for this need to be fully considered. High levels of conflict between children and complaints about unfair or unequal treatment are also crucial to record and to address (see Appendix 2).

INTERVENING TO HELP PROMOTE BETTER PEER AND SIBLING RELATIONSHIPS – WHAT MIGHT HELP?

When children have experienced early adversity, such as poor parenting, they may not have learned core social–emotional skills during preschool years. This "gap" in their development is likely to make it harder for them to get on well with brothers and sisters, and is also likely to impact on relationships with peers.

Kalvin *et al* (2015) state that promoting social–emotional development during the pre-school years is a priority and that in order to promote positive peer relations, pre-school programmes need to target skills associated with peer acceptance and protect against peer rejection. During the pre-school years, these skills include:

- co-operative play skills (taking turns, sharing toys, collaborating in pretend play and responding positively to peers);

- language and communication skills (conversing with peers, suggesting and elaborating joint play themes, asking questions and responding to requests for clarification, inviting others to play);

- emotional understanding and regulation (identifying the feelings of self and others, regulating affect when excited or upset, inhibiting emotional outbursts and coping with everyday frustrations); and

- aggression control and social problem-solving skills (inhibiting reactive aggression, managing conflicts verbally, generating alternative solutions and negotiating with peers).

Encouragingly, they highlight that developmental research suggests that social-emotional competencies can be taught using explicit coaching strategies that include skill explanations, demonstrations, and practice activities.

A few research studies have also evaluated interventions that can help improve sibling relationships (McBeath *et al*, 2014, Linares *et al*, 2015; Kothari *et al*, 2017; Waid and Wojciak, 2017). The interventions have generally focused on reducing conflict and aggression by, for example, teaching/coaching parents to become effective mediators. The studies provide some optimism that changes within sibling relationships *can* be facilitated through specific interventions and arguably, this should serve as an impetus for service development. A few programmes have addressed difficulties in sibling relationships; generally, these have focused on reducing conflict and aggression. Teaching children not to fight will not of itself help siblings to develop all the skills needed to interact positively with their brothers and sisters.

Findings across six regions in the US suggested that participation in the well-established Camp to Belong programme (a week-long summer camp for siblings separated in foster care) may reduce sibling conflict and help improve sibling support (Waid and Wojcaik, 2017).

In the US, Supporting Siblings in Foster Care (SIBS-FC), a 12-session relationship enhancement intervention, has been used with sibling pairs aged 7–15 living together or separately in out of home care (Kothari *et al*, 2017). SIBS-FC was recently reviewed (Waid *et al*, 2021) to examine if there were critical components of the intervention that were associated with changes to sibling relationship quality. Waid *et al* identified that "positive sib thinking" was particularly helpful. This component includes: noticing positive things and strengths even when times are hard (e.g. something the child/young person is proud of, or hopes and dreams for the future); and positive affirmations about self and about a sibling (something positive and true). Coaches emphasised that practice was necessary to incorporate this habit as a way of being. They acknowledged hardships and discussed handling difficult situations, but encouraged participants to think about affirmations and focus on staying positive even when they felt discouraged.

There is a clear need to learn from such initiatives and to develop practices that help promote and facilitate supportive relationships between siblings. In particular, it will be important to develop strategies that can be used with much younger children placed together or apart.

With skilled input, foster carers can help provide reparative care for children. Reparative care can help children to become both more emotionally regulated and better able to understand and manage relationships with siblings and peers. A focus on improving sibling relationships should have wider positive benefits for children, and in particular will be likely to promote peer relationships. These relationships are also crucially important in respect of education and later life.

FOSTER CARERS AND SEPARATED SIBLINGS – PLACEMENT AND CONTACT ISSUES

When children are placed apart, their foster carers will need to know the reasons for this so that they can support children and help them to understand what is happening and why. Foster carers have a major role in helping children to maintain family relationships and have been described as the "gatekeepers" of sibling contact (James *et al*, 2008, p99). Training and support regarding sibling contact and the positive effects this may have on a child's development and sense of identity are crucial elements to address. The role of foster carers in facilitating contact /family time with the child's siblings may involve providing transport, making practical arrangements, encouraging contact with the child's birth family as well as supporting the child emotionally. Where there might be risks or safeguarding concerns, they should be openly acknowledged and discussed with relevant professionals.

Social workers should ensure that key information about children's behaviour, routines and any special requirements is shared with the children's respective foster carers. **The foster carers should be involved in planning contact /family time and know what is expected, when and by whom**; for example, a contact plan should ideally include some regular overnight stays unless there are reasons to preclude this. The children's foster carers may already know each other and be able to work well together but this should not be assumed. A planning meeting should be held so that expectations and needs can be addressed. The children's foster carers should have opportunities to discuss how they will manage behaviours, for example, recognising that siblings' roles may be distorted and that safe care practices will need to be in place. Some foster carers will be better able to facilitate contact in their home than elsewhere. Factors such as accommodation, work commitments and the needs of other children at home should be considered. Practical and financial support issues must also be addressed. The importance of foster carers providing feedback about contact and contributing written observations to inform assessments should also be discussed at an early stage (see Appendix 2).

Most children will benefit from a visit to see where other siblings are living and this can provide much-needed reassurance. An opportunity to see a sibling's bedroom and to know who is looking after a much-loved brother or sister may help children to settle. Meeting foster carers who are looking after brothers and sisters living elsewhere is also likely to be reassuring. Such visits should usually be planned as soon as possible, unless safeguarding reasons preclude this from happening. Photos and knowing that more visits will happen soon are also important in helping children to manage separation anxiety.

Research has shown that despite the vital role that foster carers play, they can often have mixed feelings about contact with siblings. They may not understand what the reasons are for maintaining contact – they may fear the upset that it may cause to the child, find managing the practical aspects difficult or see no benefit from the contact. Carers may need additional training and support to understand the significance of contact and its vital importance for most children. Having an understanding of why children may behave in certain ways can help, for example, carers learning more about factors that influence the quality of sibling relationships. When siblings are separated, contact, including overnight visits, may allow crucial opportunities for reparative work with brothers and sisters.

Whatever the level of contact and wherever it takes place, foster carers should be asked to provide feedback on the impact that this appears to have on each child. In some instances, sibling visits may take place at one of the foster carer's homes; alternatively, children may meet at a contact centre and their time together be supervised, or the children's respective foster carers may all meet up at a park or play facility. A range of contacts may take place such that foster carers may be present throughout the visit or only see a child before and afterwards. Foster carers should be asked to share their observations by providing written feedback that might include some or all of the following elements:

- how the child appeared prior to seeing their siblings (for example, were they content/happy/excited/wary/upset?);

- how the children interacted (for example, who played together, examples of shared fun and any difficult behaviours or fall-outs);

- how the child appeared after contact (for example, fine, no significant differences observed/seemed more excitable than usual/was upset/was more defiant);

- any other issues or comments they may like to note. See Appendix 2 for forms to record these.

KEY PRACTICE POINTS

- Those involved in caring for and working with the sibling group should meet to draw up a written plan for family time, including visits and maintaining links between the children. This should happen at the earliest opportunity and at least prior to the first review. The plan should ensure clarity about the level of contact that can be managed between the foster carers and what will be arranged by the social workers involved.

- Children should see each other outside of parental family time. In particular, they should have regular opportunities to talk and play, to share meals and help one another.

- Plans should address overnight contact, allowing separated siblings to go to bed and wake up in the same house on at least some occasions; for example, consideration should be given to foster carers taking it in turns to have the whole sibling group for a weekend perhaps once every two or three weeks.

- Practical and financial support to carers needs to be addressed so that this is not an obstacle when planning and promoting contact between brothers and sisters.

- Foster carers' observations on the impact of contact, including visits between brothers and sisters, is routinely sought. A semi-structured form for use with carers is provided in Appendix 2.

WORK WITH THE CHILDREN – PHOTOS, EXPLANATIONS AND VISITS

It is important that children know the reasons for the plan that is made for them. The plan should be explained to them in a way that they can understand, with opportunities to ask questions and to say what they think and feel. In the absence of accurate information and clear explanations, children may harbour anger and potentially blame themselves or a sibling. Explanations are crucial in helping children and young people to understand why they are in care and why they might be separated from their siblings, if this has to happen. In particular, it is more helpful for a child to know if separation has taken place simply because there wasn't a foster home available to care for them and their siblings, rather than to worry that separation was because of something they or a sibling might have said or done. In a recent study that canvassed looked after children's views on their well-being, nearly one-third of four- to seven-year-olds thought that they did not have a good understanding of why they were in care (Selwyn and Briheim-Crookall, 2017).

Being given an explanation of why things happen can help to reduce feelings of powerlessness. Children entering care are likely to experience a sense that they are passive victims in an adult process. This heightens the responsibility on the part of adults to ensure that the child understands that their views are always being thought about. Knowing that your voice is heard and your feelings recognised is linked to increased well-being and better mental health.

Ensuring that children keep in touch with one another is a priority and they will benefit from knowing that this is also a priority for you, as their social worker:

> *Maintaining contact with siblings (from both the same or different parents) is reported by children to be one of their highest priorities. It can provide continuity and stability for a child in a time of uncertainty and possibly great change. Sibling contact can help a child maintain their identity in an unfamiliar environment and promote self-esteem and emotional support.*
>
> (*Children Act 1989 Guidance And Regulations Volume 2: Care planning, placement and case review*, as updated July 2015, para 2.85)

Unless there are clear safeguarding reasons to preclude a child having a continuing relationship with siblings, it is important to think about what will help when they are placed apart. Children will benefit from knowing why this happened and from achieving a sense that, despite this having happened, their relationships are still very much valued and will be supported.

KEY PRACTICE POINTS

- Complete a diary or use a pictorial calendar and stickers with a young child to ensure that they and their carers know the dates of brothers' and sisters' birthdays.

- Ensure that each child has photos (and film material wherever possible) of brothers and sisters and that this is accessible: for example, children may want to view photos on the foster carer's computer and some older children may wish to access photos on their mobile phone.

- Ensure that each child knows when they will see their brothers and sisters and think about how they can exercise some choice, for example, over location and activities.

- Ensure that children are able to contact brothers and sisters living elsewhere by phone, video call or other appropriate means, either freely or on a planned basis with adult support.

- Ensure that children have an opportunity to visit the foster home where their brothers and sisters live and that they are able to see their siblings' bedroom and meet their foster carers.

THE QUALITY OF CONTACT – OBSERVATIONS AND LINKS TO ASSESSMENT

Children spending family time together without their parents or other adult relatives may not receive the priority it should, and yet it is both key to children's well-being and can helpfully inform assessments. Notably, Monk and Macvarish (2020) found that the significance of sibling relationships was routinely outweighed by other assumptions in decision-making within care proceedings – for example, the idea that placement stability would be disrupted through sibling contact, or that maintaining birth parent contact is a higher priority than sibling contact.

Contact between separated brothers and sisters is not only important for children in its own right but can also provide rich opportunities to learn more about how a child relates to each of their siblings. It is helpful to think about how behaviour and interactions during contact are recorded and ideally this should commence as soon as children become looked after. The importance of involving foster carers and obtaining feedback from them has been addressed earlier in this chapter. Forms for recording contact observations need to include appropriate headings so that information can not only be noted at the time but can be more easily extracted and collated subsequently. Suggestions about the issues that should be addressed are set out in the forms available in Appendix 2.

Staff undertaking contact supervision need to know what aspects should be observed and recorded during each session. Their focus may primarily be on observing interactions between parents and children but child-to-child interactions are also important. Patterns that are observed during contact can provide important pointers and examples of behaviour that may be used as supporting evidence in assessments, including sibling assessments. Having arrangements in place to aggregate information and summarise contacts on a monthly basis is particularly helpful during court proceedings. For example, a monthly summary might include details as illustrated below:

> *February:*
>
> *Mother attended five out of the eight sessions offered.*
>
> *Mother was late for three of the five sessions she attended.*
>
> *Mother brought snacks to each session as recommended.*
>
> *Mother used her mobile phone in each session despite the written agreement that she should not do so.*
>
> *Key theme: Mother continues to show preferential treatment towards Preston. For example, she always greets Preston first with a cuddle whilst his sisters typically stand impassively waiting for their mum's attention. During contact time overall, mother is less affectionate towards Charmaine and Lucy, who have each shown resentment towards Preston, for example, calling him a "pooh head" and trying to shove him out of the way if he sometimes tries to join their play activity. When Preston hits his sisters (note: this occurred during all the sessions observed), mother does not take any action. Mother consistently lets Preston choose his favourite drink or snack (e.g. strawberry yoghurt from a multi-flavoured pack) which has led to squeals and angry outbursts – verbal and physical – from both his sisters. This behaviour was particularly concerning in the sessions held on 3 and 16 February.*

KEY PRACTICE POINTS

Use a form (see Appendix 2) for recording that includes dedicated questions and space to note interactions between parents and children, and brothers and sisters. This can help foster carers and contact supervisors to identify:

- the ways in which a parent or relative behaves towards each child in a sibling group;

- differential treatment by a parent or relative of one or more children;
- patterns of interaction between brothers and sisters.

Contact supervisors may need, or benefit from, additional training. This should focus on aspects that are especially important to observe and record in respect of sibling interactions and behaviour.

Work with other professionals – information about brothers and sisters

Health visitors and education staff (including pre-school) may have important knowledge about the children's sibling relationships but may not be routinely asked to contribute to sibling assessments. It is helpful to think about whom to contact and when to do so in order to access information that might influence planning. Forms and letters to use with health and education staff are provided in Appendix 2.

KEY MESSAGES

Policy questions to consider

Strategic planning that takes account of siblings is likely to impact on the availability of resources as well as the services provided. For example:

- Are the additional issues involved in meeting the needs of sibling groups considered, identified and then embedded in planning?
- Do you have detailed information about placement patterns relating to sibling groups?
- Do you know what is being done well but also remain alert to gaps in service provision?
- Do recruitment drives for foster carers or adopters highlight the need to keep siblings together as well as the support that will be provided to facilitate this?
- Do staff have the necessary training, skills and experience in working with and assessing siblings? Are examples of good practice shared?
- Are foster carers provided with sufficient support to enable them to constructively manage both the practical and family/relationship issues presented when caring for siblings?
- Is it possible to introduce the use of SDQs for children early on, and in particular for children in sibling groups where one or more children are aged three and above?

Practice issues

- Children who are living apart from some or all of their siblings know why this happened and have a shared age-appropriate understanding of why they all came into care.

- Separated siblings have been able to visit the foster home/s where their brothers and sisters live.

- Separated siblings have photos of their family and in particular of brothers and sisters. They also have access to important information such as dates of birthdays and family visits.

- Children and their foster carers have a clear understanding of how sibling relationships will be supported and promoted.

- Information about the children's past and current sibling relationships is actively sought.

- SDQs are completed early on with foster carers and education staff for children aged three and above (see Chapter 5 for more detail on the benefits of using SDQs).

- Observations of contact sessions involving the children and/or their parents should include aspects relevant to children's sibling relationships. Contact supervisors should be aware of factors that are important to identify, such as differential treatment and affection shown by parents or wider family (see Appendix 2).

Chapter 4
Frameworks for the assessment of sibling relationships and placements

INTRODUCTION

This chapter provides a brief overview of frameworks that have been used in practice for the assessment of sibling relationships and placements. Some of the frameworks are quite detailed, whilst others suggest key domains that are important to consider in assessing the relationships between brothers and sisters, including factors that might indicate separate placements. Chapter 5, on assessment, describes the approach that is recommended in this guide and sometimes refers to key elements that have been commonly identified as important within this chapter.

VARIOUS FRAMEWORKS, MODELS AND APPROACHES

Furman and Buhrmester (1985) suggested that four key dimensions are relevant when assessing sibling relationships:

- the degree of warmth;
- the degree of conflict;
- the degree of rivalry;
- the degree to which a child nurtures or dominates another sibling.

Kosonen (1996) wrote about factors in the birth family that can negatively influence the relationship between siblings. These include the following:

- poor attachments to parents, which can result in intense sibling conflict;

- a conflictual relationship between parents, which can also result in poor sibling relationships, with a tendency for boys to be particularly affected;

- parental favouritism is likely to increase sibling conflict and to be negative for both favoured and non-favoured children. However, if children can perceive differential treatment as "fair", their sibling relationships need not suffer;

- neglect and parental unavailability can result in strong compensatory sibling relationships, particularly if an older sibling provides some parenting of younger children. However, in the absence of parental care and supervision, these sibling bonds may become abusive and/or result in unmet needs;

- the impact of abuse: this may result in poor and hostile sibling relationships for both abused and non-abused children. Children who have been abused may be particularly resentful of those who have not;

- "high access" siblings, i.e. those close in age and of the same sex, can have an emotionally intense relationship with high levels of conflict;

- the impact of non-shared environment: it is important to remember that no two siblings will have exactly the same experience, either in their relationships with other family members or with those outside the family, such as other relatives, teachers, friends, etc. These individual factors can have an important effect on how each child relates to siblings.

The **Department of Health** publication, *Patterns and Outcomes in Child Placement* (1991), included checklists as a basic tool for studying the way in which siblings behaved towards each other. These focused on the assessment of sibling pairs, but did not consider the dynamics of larger groups of brothers and sisters. The text noted the importance of recording behaviour and understanding the context in which this had developed, suggesting that the following aspects were significant:

- the child's position in the family;

- the sex of the children;

- the "cultural and family expectations" for each child;

- the emotional age at which each child is functioning;

- the extent to which children have a shared history and family experience;

- the role each child is perceived to have played (if any) in the sibling group's admission to care or accommodation.

The Department of Health Sibling Checklists have been used by practitioners in many assessments in recent years. Lord and Borthwick (2008) described the importance of a considered and nuanced approach to assessments and the work required with brothers and sisters to determine whether they should be placed together or apart. In practice, however, the Department of Health Sibling Checklist has sometimes been used in an overly simplistic way.

In **Together or Apart** (Lord and Borthwick, 2008, p20), Gerrilyn Smith is quoted in her provision of a summary of circumstances that may indicate that siblings should be placed separately:

- *intense rivalry and jealousy, with each child totally preoccupied with, and unable to tolerate the attention which their sibling(s) may be getting;*
- *exploitation, often based on gender, e.g. boys may have been seen (in their birth family) and see themselves as inherently superior to their sisters, with a right to dominate and exploit them;*
- *chronic scapegoating of one child;*
- *maintaining unhelpful alliances in a sibling group and family-of-origin conflicts – sibling patterns of behaviour may be strongly entrenched and may prevent re-parenting or learning new cultural norms;*
- *maintaining unhelpful hierarchical positions, e.g. a child may be stuck in the role of victim or bully;*
- *highly sexualised behaviour with each other;*
- *acting as triggers to each other's traumatic material and potentially constantly re-traumatising each other. The triggers may well be unconscious, unintentional and mundane.*

In **Ten Top Tips on Placing Siblings**, Argent (2008, p32) grappled with the complexity of understanding how siblings related to one another and suggested the following were important issues to consider:

- *How does the group deal with stress in the family, how do the siblings deal with conflict within the group, how does each individual child react to pressure?*
- *Do siblings recognise each other's distress and support and comfort each other, do they close ranks against outsiders?*
- *If individual children get pushed out because they have hurt or upset brothers and sisters, are they able to rejoin the group?*
- *Does any one child take responsibility, or blame, for the actions of all?*
- *Can each child express feelings and wishes, or is there a spokesperson?*
- *Who initiates play? Is play boisterous and pleasurable or competitive and aggressive?*
- *Which children "gang up", "pair off" and which appear to be "loners"?*
- *How and to whom do individual children show affection?*
- *Who irritates, teases or tries to get others into trouble?*

- *Who shares secrets, interests, or copies each other's behaviour?*
- *Do children assume distinguishable roles? How do siblings describe each other?*
- *How does each child rank in the sibling group and gain the attention of adults?*

She also suggested that the Strengths and Difficulties Questionnaire (SDQ) (Goodman, 1997) was helpful when assessing individual children within a sibling group.

Groza *et al* (2003, p486) described a multi-dimensional assessment tool for making decisions regarding the placement of siblings, using the following framework:

Description of sibling relationship

- Type/degree
- Duration
- Intensity
- Quality

Safety issues

- Risk factors
- Context of risk factors
- Services/interventions employed to reduce or effectively manage risk
- Response to services/interventions

Benefits experienced by the children for keeping siblings together

- *Children do not have to experience another loss (can begin to heal).*
- *Children have a shared history (sense of roots).*
- *Children learn to work through their problems rather than running from them.*
- *Children feel safe in a new home when they are with siblings.*
- *Children are better able to attach to caregivers when the sibling attachment has not been damaged.*
- *Children have other people in the family who look after them.*
- *Children have a shared biological/genetic history that can be used to predict future physical/medical needs based on the eldest child.*

Benefits of separating siblings

- *The child is living with a family that they have resided with for a significant period of time and has formed an attachment; moving then will result in significant loss.*

- *The child will be physically and emotionally safer remaining separated.*

- *The child has such special needs that separating him or her will allow the family to meet those needs.*

Children's wishes and expectations should also be sought, alongside the availability of suitable families.

The **Family Futures** assessment handbook (2007, updated 2019) outlines their approach. This framework looks at four key elements in assessing the sibling relationships of fostered or adopted children:

- the parenting intensity that is needed by each child (the degree of developmental trauma experienced by looked after children means that they often require very intensive developmental re-parenting);

- the nature of the sibling relationship (parenting siblings who have been harmed by earlier experiences and whose sibling relationships have been pathologised can be very demanding, and managing such relationships should not be allowed to jeopardise developing a secure attachment between child and parent);

- the compatibility of the siblings' parenting needs (the variety of sibling needs may make it hard for a parent to exercise one consistent parenting style across the group);

- the security of the sibling attachment relationship.

Each child is rated as high, medium or low on each dimension.

The handbook outlines an approach to analysing sibling relationships based on the work of Jaak Panksepp (1998), noting that:

> *From his extensive research on rats, he has determined that there are four main systems in the primitive brain which are essential for survival and are activated by attachment behaviour. These systems are common to animals and humans alike, they are: Aggression, Fear, Comfort seeking and Play.*

Family Futures suggests that this framework can be applied to observations of children, particularly young children who have experienced early trauma, and suggests that:

> *Rating a child as high, medium or low on each dimension in terms of the level of activation of each of these four systems can lead to an assessment of the security of the sibling attachment relationships. In this model, secure attachment behaviour is represented as exhibiting medium levels of aggression and fearful behaviour since these*

behaviours are adaptive and essential for survival. Comfort seeking and playful behaviour are also at medium levels of activation as they too are adaptive and linked to survival and development of the animal or person. Play in this context refers to normal age-appropriate interactive play, e.g. rough and tumble, hide'n'seek, chasing, etc. In contrast, traumatised children may exhibit high levels of play but the play will be traumatised and characterised by repetition, ritual, violence and scary themes. When played out between children, it is not reciprocal and collaborative; instead domination, power and control are characteristic of the interaction as it is a re-enactment of unresolved traumatic experience.

For more information, see *Siblings Together or Apart*, available at: www.familyfutures.co.uk/wp-content/uploads/2015/05/Siblings-Together-or-Apart-Practice-Paper.compressed.pdf.

Note: It is important to consider the context within which this framework developed. Family Futures is a registered voluntary adoption agency (VAA) based in London, and places a small number of children with highly complex needs (in 2016, the agency placed six children), provides adoption support to many more families and training for both families and practitioners. The agency is well-established and well-regarded; however, it is also important to note that families who access its support may not be typical and the children not representative of the wider pool of brothers and sisters placed for adoption.

More generally, be clear about the language you use and any research underpinning your assessment. Also, be aware that you may be criticised if you cannot provide a clear account of how you reached your conclusions and recommendations – including in court. See, for example, Shemmings (2016, 2018). Further information is provided on this in Chapter 5.

Farnfield (2009) described a modified Strange Situation Procedure for use in assessing sibling relationships and their attachment to carers. He made a number of suggestions considered crucial to understanding sibling relationships. The Strange Situation is the method of assessing attachment styles originally developed by Mary Ainsworth (Ainsworth *et al*, 1969). The modified procedure for use with siblings requires a standard video suite with observation room and one-way screen. A selection of toys should be available for the children. All parts of the assessment are recorded on video. The procedure has been used with children ranging in age from three years and five months, up to 12 years.

It is designed to be used in conjunction with other sources of information. Further research on the degree of correspondence with children's behaviour in other settings is needed before it can be validated and this would require home and school observations over time. In addition, the model is not developed in a social work setting and appears to be in the context of specialist assessment outside the domain of local authority decision-making. To date, there has been no systematic validation study of this procedure in a social work setting (see Dibben *et al*, 2018).

Note: It is important to be clear about whether you have the appropriate training to undertake this, and if not, to be aware that you may be criticised – including in court, as highlighted by Shemmings (2016, 2018) and discussed further in Chapter 5.

Kramer (2010) provided a list of criteria for judging the quality of prosocial sibling relationships, including the following aspects:

- positive engagement;
- cohesion;
- shared experiences that build support;
- social and emotional understanding;
- perspective taking;
- emotional regulation and behavioural control;
- forming neutral or positive attributions;
- conflict management and problem-solving;
- responding to parental differential treatment.

The US publication, **Sibling Issues in Foster Care and Adoption**, by the Child Welfare Information Gateway (2013, p9) suggests that:

> *In completing assessments, it is important to recognise that sibling relationships vary greatly in both positive and negative qualities. In evaluating the quality of sibling relationships, the worker will want to look for warmth or affection between siblings, rivalry and hostility, interdependence, and relative power and status in the relationship, as well as determining how much time the siblings have spent together.*

Staff undertaking assessments are encouraged to be aware of bias, to talk with children individually and ask age-appropriate questions, such as:

- *Which sibling do you enjoy spending time with?*
- *Which sibling enjoys spending time with you?*
- *Who will play a game with you?*
- *Which sibling do you turn to when you are afraid or hurt?*
- *Which sibling turns to you when he or she is afraid or hurt?*

DISCUSSION – FRAMEWORKS

As Dibben *et al* (2018, p9) recently concluded:

- *There is an absence of any published formal measures or tools developed directly in the context of social work practice that have been validated. This is an area for further longitudinal research.*

- *The majority of tools available have been developed with samples that are not in the context of work with siblings who have suffered trauma or abuse.*

- *There are few measures that can be utilised with younger children and infants under five, albeit that this is the main population of siblings in the context of adoption work.*

- *There is a gap in social workers' understanding of how to assess larger sibling group dynamics and understand sibling relationships in the context of wider, influential family relationships.*

Clearly there is a range of different frameworks available for you to consider using in your assessment of sibling relationships; however, all of them have some limitations. There is no simple answer. The approach that is recommended within this guide is that you should have an awareness of the frameworks and why some aspects are important to address.

KEY PRACTICE POINTS

- The Department of Health Sibling Checklists (1991) have been used by practitioners in the UK for many assessments. These checklists focused on the assessment of sibling pairs, but did not consider the dynamics of larger groups of brothers and sisters. There may have been an over-reliance on the checklists, especially when used in an overly simplistic way rather than as a small part of a nuanced assessment.

- There are a range of other frameworks and publications that are helpful to consider but all have some limitations. Despite these, there is some common ground. For example, frameworks generally include some recognition that the following elements are important to consider:

  - warmth and positive engagement, the level of care shown by a child towards their sibling/s;

  - conflict and aggressive behaviour, including attempts to dominate, bully or undermine a sibling;

  - the extent to which siblings compete and show rivalry for adult attention.

- Our knowledge base about what influences sibling relationships has grown and we now understand much more about factors such as high conflict between brothers and sisters. Similarly, our knowledge base about the impact of such behaviours on placement outcomes is now more sophisticated. It is crucial for assessment tools and frameworks to encompass these and other key elements.

These issues are addressed in depth in the next chapter on assessment.

Chapter 5
Assessment: what you should include and why

INTRODUCTION

The aim of this chapter is to encourage a structured, coherent approach to the assessment of siblings that builds on existing knowledge and includes a range of perspectives. There is consideration of what is required and what might helpfully be included within a comprehensive sibling assessment. Tools that may be helpful to consider, questions and ideas for working with family members, children and their carers are set out. The importance of involving professionals from other settings, notably health and education, is also stressed; health visitors, for example, often have helpful observations to contribute about the development of children and their relationships with brothers and sisters. Appendix 2 contains a range of forms that you may use for this or adapt.

Some of the key points noted here have been emphasised in earlier sections of this guide, so to some extent the work that you need to undertake now will partly depend on what has already been done and whether, for example, you have access to information that was sought as part of the early planning suggestions recommended in Chapter 3. As set out in *Working Together* (Department for Education, 2018b, p25), assessment is a dynamic process that should analyse and respond to changing need and risk. The Department for Education helpfully states that:

> *It is important that the impact of what is happening to a child is clearly identified and that information is gathered, recorded and checked systematically, and discussed with the child and their parents/carers where appropriate.*

Some of the hallmarks of high quality assessments identified are that they are: child-centred; holistic; focused on action and outcomes; involve children and families and build on strengths as well as identifying difficulties; are multi-agency and multi-disciplinary; and are transparent and open to challenge. All of these elements are central when assessing brothers and sisters for permanent placements.

When reaching a decision as to whether or not brothers and sisters should be placed together for adoption, statutory guidance calls for:

> *A comprehensive assessment of the quality of the children's relationship, their individual needs and the likely capacity of the prospective adopter to meet the needs of all the siblings being placed together.*
>
> (Department for Education, 2013)

It is crucial to conduct a full assessment of each child in a sibling group as well as an assessment of their relationships with one another. Even if it seems clear that the brothers and sisters should remain together, a detailed assessment will provide essential information for a new family and will enable the agency to anticipate the extra help and support that may be necessary. Equally, if it is determined that children are to be separated or to remain apart, the reasons for this should be made clear and reports should fully explore issues in respect of contact and how relationships can be promoted. The benefits of different placement options and combinations require a careful balancing exercise and this is likely to be especially challenging in respect of sibling groups where children have intense and divergent parenting needs, where the age span is greater, and when older children may have significant, complex relationships with some birth relatives. The extent to which contact is actively considered and supported within the range of permanency options is also likely to influence what placement options are perceived as viable within each authority. Practice may vary significantly in this regard. Some adoption agencies are more encouraging and broadly supportive of contact than others, whilst some may be more cautious and "risk averse" (see Chapter 9).

Children and young people should be involved and feel involved, and those who know them well should be similarly engaged in the assessment. Early engagement and active participation should make it easier for adults to understand the outcome, be more likely to accept reasons for decisions, and be better equipped to support children and young people to develop a coherent narrative in the years ahead. The assessment process should "feed into" explanations and information, with key elements being included in life story work and more detailed accounts provided in later life letters for children and young people.

The previous chapter summarised different frameworks and approaches that have addressed issues specific to sibling assessments. However, although you may consider using some of them, it is important to recognise their limitations. There is no simple answer or shortcut in this field.

ASSESSMENT: KEY ELEMENTS AND RATIONALE

The approach to assessment that is recommended within this guide is very much a partnership, step-by-step approach based on an understanding of what we have learned from research as well as the experiences of children and families. Several dimensions are clearly important to address, for example, the frameworks reviewed in the last chapter generally include some recognition that the following elements are especially relevant:

- warmth and positive engagement, the level of care shown by a child towards their sibling/s;

- conflict and aggressive behaviour, including attempts to dominate, bully or undermine a sibling;

- the extent to which siblings compete and show rivalry for adult attention.

Our enhanced understanding of the experiences of children and adoptive families, together with research on outcomes, is also key. We now know more about the impact of pre-placement experiences and should strive to fully take account of each child's emotional and behavioural needs. Particularly high levels of behavioural difficulties presented by one or more children may understandably lead us to worry about placing them all together or in a particular combination – even if there is also evidence of emotional warmth between the siblings.

When thinking about research on placement outcomes, we need to remain focused on the fact that research relates to populations of children and as such is probabilistic and not deterministic; in general terms, though, we know that some factors increase risks:

- Age is important – children who are older when they join their new family tend to have fewer good outcomes when compared with populations of younger-placed children.

- Higher levels of maltreatment are significant – children's pre-placement experiences are more significant than age at placement on its own. "Good start-late placed" older children may have better outcomes than younger children who were exposed to particularly high levels of adversity and low levels of emotional warmth (Howe, 1998).

- Children who have been exposed to drugs or alcohol *in utero* are likely to be at greater risk (Neil *et al*, 2018).

- Adopted children who have experienced delays in decision-making are more likely to experience a disruption than those for whom planning is more timely (Selwyn *et al*, 2014).

- Children who spend more than 12 months in care are likely to be at risk (Neil *et al*, 2018).

- Children who have two or more foster homes before moving to their adoptive family are likely to be at risk (Neil *et al*, 2018).

- Children placed over the age of four years old are more likely to experience disruption (Selwyn *et al*, 2014).

- Aggression and violence are the most frequently described forms of challenging behaviour identified by adopters and become more difficult to manage during adolescence (Selwyn *et al*, 2014).

In essence, then, when conducting sibling assessments and making plans for each child, we need to consider:

- each child's experiences within their birth family;

- each child's experiences in care;

- each child's individual needs;

- each child's relationship with their brothers and sisters.

Values, attitudes and experiences

It is helpful to think about your starting point and your own value base: do you feel strongly about whether brothers or sisters should stay together? To what extent might your own views have been shaped by your personal and professional experience, or experiences of others within your team? Research has found that social workers may be more influenced by experience of disruptions than stories of success and the positive placement of brothers and sisters (Dibben *et al*, 2018). It is inevitably the case that our individual experience and those of others involved will have some impact, so it is important to hold this in mind, to be reflective, remaining open to both learning and challenge. Social workers tell us that undertaking sibling assessments is a daunting responsibility. Multi-sourcing observations, sharing good practice, considering research on placement outcomes and having space to reflect within supervision can all help make the task more manageable and contribute to better outcomes for children.

Say what you see and also include what others see

The importance of providing a clear account of your own observations, and describing behaviours and the context in which you saw them, should be at the heart of your assessment. Your own observations should be supplemented and supported by additional observations made by foster carers and others who know the children well. Where there are significant discrepancies between observations and views, it is crucial to interrogate them, that is, consider what might account for these differences.

ASSESSMENT: WHAT YOU SHOULD INCLUDE AND WHY

Shemmings (2018) cited and commented on a court case where a judge had criticised a social work witness statement for being long on rhetoric and criticism but short on concrete examples of where and how the mother's parenting had been deficient. During oral evidence, when asked to provide examples, the social workers had struggled to do so.

Whilst a good understanding of attachment theory and research will helpfully inform practice, Shemmings (2018) reminds social workers of the training required to become fully accredited in assessing attachments and strongly recommends that they substitute the word "relationship" instead. He also advised practitioners to:

> ...take heed of Professor Sue White's tip to 'say what you see'. Of course, that may assume that we all see the same thing but if we then expose fully what assumptions we are making, including the use of theory, then we remain accountable, both to the court and to family members.

STRUCTURING AND MANAGING THE PROCESS – WHAT A COHERENT ASSESSMENT MIGHT INCLUDE

In the section on early planning in Chapter 3, some key steps that help facilitate assessment work and share tasks appropriately were set out. It is helpful to review what information you already have and what actions you need to take now.

Think about how you will structure your assessment: what information and observations you might contribute directly and what contributions you can seek from others. The assessment report headings below are intended to provide a guide to key elements that you might helpfully and commonly include and some of which you will already have access to.

Key elements in an assessment report

- Key background information.
- Details of each child in the sibling group.
- Details of social worker.
- Work undertaken to complete the report.
- Key background information and impact on children's sibling relationship.
- The views of parents and significant relatives.
- Key observations of the children and their sibling relationship.

- Findings from SDQ.
- Overview of each child and their individual needs.
- Overview of sibling relationships.
- Support or interventions provided re: the sibling relationship.
- Consideration of realistic placement options.
- Analysis and recommendation re: placement.
- Consideration of and recommendations for contact.
- Recommendations for future support.
- Signatures and date report completed.

Working through each of the key elements above should help you build a comprehensive report that is robust and helpful in a range of settings and in different ways: in court, and for explanations to children, family members and future adopters/carers.

You may have worked with the children prior to them entering care and have been able to follow many of the suggestions set out earlier in this guide, or your involvement may be much more recent. The actions that you need to take now will clearly depend on what assessment work has already been undertaken. Ensure that you use information and evidence that is already available, and be clear about what further work and observations you may now need to complete.

Plan your assessment, such that on completion it will include information from a range of sources and people. You may decide to use or adapt some of the forms in Appendix 2 or you or your local authority may decide to develop your own. The important thing is that observations are sought about each child and their sibling relationships and that there is a focus on both positive and any concerning or negative aspects. Sending forms by email for completion by each contributor and allowing them sufficient time to respond is an efficient way of managing the work, which should also enhance the quality of the overall assessment. Some carers may need support and assistance from their supervising social worker to complete these, especially if this is the first time that they have contributed to a sibling assessment.

Key background information, chronologies, early parenting and adversity

In addition to your own "working knowledge" of a family, a lot of information about children and their relationships with brothers and sisters may be held on case files – perhaps recorded by previous social care staff – whilst other information will be held by professionals who know the family. How easy this is to "retrieve" and whether you routinely seek the views of others are key elements to consider now.

Local authorities are encouraged to develop a chronology template that includes a focus on sibling relationships, unless this is already established practice. Chronologies can provide a rich overview of information about children's experiences and can help workers trace, consider and review significant events. They have the potential to provide much helpful information if details about siblings are recorded and highlighted. For example:

- early attachment relationships;
- the impact of the birth of a new child on existing children in the family;
- parental behaviour towards each child and any observed impacts (for example, noting differential treatment of one or more children);
- clarity about any episodes a child has spent apart from siblings and reasons for these;
- observations regarding how a child interacts with his or her siblings.

Chronologies should include key points in respect of the care that each child has received as well as any periods when children have lived apart. For example, understanding the reasons why one child may have remained with their mother whilst others were cared for by grandparents may provide important clues about maternal preferential treatment, or explain that separation may have occurred for other reasons.

Chronologies can also be useful in helping you to draw up a list of whom you might contact to seek their views. For example, apart from identifying key people currently involved, you may be able to identify those with previous involvement who might shed further light on how and why behaviours developed. Crucially, this should include contacting previous carers, including family members, to obtain their observations about the child or children whom they looked after.

Parenting assessments will contain important information about the children's experiences and any early adversity that they may have experienced individually and collectively. It will be crucial to consider the impact of this within your assessment. See Chapters 4 and 10 for an overview of relevant research.

Using a range of sources of information and identifying how and when behaviours started will help make your overall assessment far more robust. Assessments that build on each child's history and use information from a range of professionals will also make it far easier to explain how and why you have reached a particular decision. This will not only be helpful during court proceedings but importantly provides key information for life story work and later life letters. CoramBAAF has various guides on life story work and also one on writing later life letters (see Useful Resources).

Parents and relatives' views about the children and their sibling relationships

Talk to parents – and significant relatives – about each child, and actively seek their views about how relationships developed between brothers and sisters. Parenting assessments should already include information about siblings, so review this and think about what aspects you can usefully summarise to include in your sibling assessment.

The way in which a child might be regarded by one or both parents as well as by their wider family may be significant, for example, has one or more of the children been treated negatively when compared with other siblings? In discussions with parents, seek their views about their children's sibling relationships: some key "starter" questions you might use with the children's mother include: Was A a planned child? How did you feel when you were expecting A? How did A's name get chosen? What was life like for you around the time of A's birth? How easy/difficult was it for you? How did A (the first-born child) respond to the birth of B (second-born child)? Did A like to help, like to hold B, or did A not take much notice of B? (And similarly, for each subsequent child born into the family unit.)

An expanded list of questions is provided in Appendix 2.

Build on the trigger questions until you have an initial overview for each child born into the family.

The questions can be adapted and used when interviewing the children's father and some of them may be helpful when speaking to relatives who know the children well.

Exploring roles and any differential treatment

Key questions to think about might include some or all of the following:

- In some families, boys are treated differently to girls – what was it like in your own family when you were growing up? What is important/what is it like in your family now?
- As a mum/dad, how do you want your boys to grow up? How do you want them to be? What is important/what is valued in your family?
- As a mum/dad, how do you want your girls to grow up? How do you want them to be? What is important/what is valued in your family?
- Some people think that boys need to be tough to cope: that by the time they start school they should be able to fight back if someone hurts

them. What do you think? What about girls, is it the same for them or different?

- Some people say that if you are too soft with boys it just makes life harder for them later on, like when they start school. What do you think?

- Is it good to treat boys and girls the same? Or is it better to treat them differently in some ways?

- In some families, girls might be expected to do more to help around the house. What do you think is best?

- In some families, girls help more with looking after younger children. In other families, it may depend on age, with the older children helping with the younger ones. What do you think is best?

- Who is most like you in your family? In what ways?

- Some children might show you that they want kisses and cuddles, for example, they might climb up on to your lap or reach out to you. Who is most likely to want cuddles from you?

- Some people think that girls are easier to parent than boys – what do you think?

- Some parents get on best with their sons/daughters. What's it like in your family?

- What about you – do you feel you have a special, very close relationship with one of your children?

- How do you know when your child, A, is upset or feeling sad? Do they show how they are feeling? (Explore for each child.)

- Sometimes the eldest child is the one who likes to "boss" the younger ones around a bit. Did this happen much at home?

Observations of the children (by social worker; foster carers; contact supervisors; education and health professionals)

As the children's social worker, you may already have considerable knowledge of each child and have seen the children together in more than one setting, or you may be relatively new to the case. Your assessment of the children's sibling relationship should build on your knowledge and include not only your own additional observations but also the observations of others who know the children, for example, foster carers, contact supervisors, education and health professionals. The use of semi-structured forms is recommended and some forms to record these are provided in Appendix 2.

Your observations of the children may already have led you to have a good understanding of interactions between them and roles within the group. In common with other assessment frameworks, practice should be "child-centred" and should include children in ways that are developmentally appropriate. The document, *Working Together to Safeguard Children* (Department for Education, 2018b, p10), sets out that:

Some of the things that children have said that they need are:

- *Vigilance: to have adults notice when things are troubling them*
- *Understanding and action: to understand what is happening; to be heard and understood; and to have that understanding acted upon*
- *Stability: to be able to develop stable, trusting relationships with those helping them*
- *Respect: to be treated with the expectation that they are competent rather than not*
- *Information and engagement: to be informed about and involved in decisions and plans*
- *Explanation: to be told about the outcome of assessments and decisions and reasons provided*
- *Support: to be provided with support in their own right*
- *Help to communicate their views.*

(Adapted from Department for Education, 2018b, p10)

Research by Selwyn and Wood (2015, p17) noted that reports tend to collect information *about* children rather than *from* children. Direct work with children, and observing brothers and sisters together and in different groups across more than one setting will not only help to make your assessment more balanced but also matters to children. Chapter 6 includes more detailed suggestions for working with children at different ages and stages.

Assessment should not only include evidence but should seek to corroborate findings throughout the process. The *Working Together* guidance (Department for Education, 2018b, p44) points out that a social worker may arrive at a judgement early on but that this may need to be revised as things change and further information comes to light:

It is a characteristic of skilled practice that social workers revisit their assumptions in the light of new evidence and take action to revise their decisions in the best interests of the individual child.

The aim is to use all the information to identify difficulties and risk factors as well as developing a picture of strengths and protective factors.

Involving children

It is important that each child in a sibling group has the opportunity for some individual sessions in which they can explore and reflect on their life at home, the reasons why they are in care, and what they would wish for in the future. This will include the opportunity for the child to express feelings about brothers and sisters, explore how much they identify with siblings, with whom they would like to live, and with whom they would like more or less contact. The potential of disabled children to communicate their wishes, feelings and views is frequently underestimated, but they may need extra help to be able to do this.

Being involved, knowing what is happening and why is important in its own right for children, but it will also help them develop a sense that they matter and their views have influence. Children and young people who feel they have some control over their lives do better educationally, are less prone to depression and anxiety and have greater resilience in the face of adversity (The Children's Society, 2015). Think about how you can help children to express their feelings about brothers and sisters, work you will undertake with them on an individual basis, and what might be helpful to do as a group.

Asking children directly which brothers or sisters they might want to be placed with is not recommended as good practice: there is no research on community samples to use as a benchmark and some children may express a view that is not salient. Children should not be given this responsibility but should be helped to express their feelings and to communicate their thoughts about family relationships.

Structure your assessment to allow opportunities to see children on their own, in different groupings and all together. Observing children at different times of the day and in different settings is also important, for example, if the eldest child is at school you may visit to allow time with pre-school siblings so that you can observe them being reunited at the end of the school day.

Each child in a sibling group should have family photos, perhaps a memory box and their own life story book. Useful work can be done with the siblings together and older children can be very helpful to younger ones in explaining what happened at home. There may be "family secrets" or different perceptions about what happened in the past that need to be addressed. Be alert to differences that are a source of conflict between children, or that provoke a profound sense of injustice, for example, one child feeling that they were treated much worse than their siblings.

Chapter 6 includes detailed ideas, suggestions and some resources that you may wish to use.

The observations of foster carers

Foster carers receive and "hold" a huge amount of rich information about children and typically, when caring for some or all of the child's siblings, they will have a great deal to contribute to assessments. The forms in Appendix 2 can be completed by foster carers to provide an overview of the following:

- each child's presentation on placement and subsequently;
- a brief summary of each child's strengths and vulnerabilities;
- information on whether the child talks about parents and family – and if so, about whom;*
- information on how each child copes with family contact;
- any significant changes that the foster carer/s have observed whilst caring for the child/ren.

Obtaining observations from foster carers that include the aspects above should provide a helpful overview. Additional elements can be added to take account of specific circumstances and needs of particular children.

The forms contained in Appendix 2 will help you to obtain a detailed picture from all those who know the children well. The foster carers' role is central here. Appendix 2 contains a form you could give to carers for them to complete over a fortnight. This provides an opportunity for carers to note interactions between the children as they arise on a daily basis. There is space for noting both positive and negative aspects of behaviour observed between the children, for example, in what ways do the children have fun and enjoy playing together? Is aggression between the siblings a source of worry? If so, what form does this take and how often does it occur? Foster carers should ideally have this form sent by secure means electronically so that they can use it flexibly, allowing as much space as needed under each of the headings. When the completed form is returned, this will also make it far easier for you to decide how best to use the information, for example, you may wish to copy key parts of their account into discrete sections of your assessment report, and/or to append the whole document at the end of your own report. The accounts provided by carers and other professionals involved will sometimes provide "different" parts of the jigsaw, and collating observations under the same heading may serve to add important emphasis to the points that you are making.

Carers should know that after you have received the completed form you will discuss their observations with them. It is relatively common for

---

* Sometimes children may not talk about their parents and family because they do not feel that it is OK to do so. It will be important to try to understand and balance the foster carer's account.

foster carers to identify arguments and some angry behaviour between some children in sibling groups. Squabbles, fall-outs and fights need to be understood and placed in context. The foster carers' observations and discussion with them about their concerns will always be important but especially so in respect of aggressive behaviour between children. Some local authorities will have direct observation tools that they recommend for recording behaviour. One simple method is an **ABC chart** that can be used to collect information in a structured way.

- **A** refers to the **antecedent**, or the event or activity that immediately precedes a problem behaviour.

- **B** refers to observed **behaviour**.

- **C** refers to the **consequence**, or the event that immediately follows a response.

Appendix 2 contains some forms and tools that can be used with foster carers to help you obtain a clearer understanding of the type, level and intensity of aggression.

Understanding when difficulties developed is also important, as is knowing if the behaviour occurs across settings, for example, is the child showing the same sort of aggression towards peers in pre-school?

When children have been placed with other foster carers previously, it will be helpful to seek their views as to the children's needs and relationships. It will always be important to understand what worked well in a foster placement and what might have been more difficult for carers to manage.

Carers and pre-school staff should also be asked to complete the appropriate SDQ for children aged three and above. The impact supplement of the SDQ should also be completed as this generates helpful information about what it is like for the carer looking after the child, as well as thinking about the child's own awareness of the difficulties that may distress him or her.

When brothers and sisters are living apart, it will be helpful to ask foster carers to complete the form (see Appendix 2) so far as is possible not only in respect of the child/ren whom they are looking after but also their observations of the children's sibling relationships based on contact visits at their home or elsewhere.

Also consider and include in your report a brief overview to help provide a context for the carers' observations. For example:

- How experienced are the foster carers and have they cared for brothers and sisters previously?

- What difficulties or challenges have they encountered?

- What support have they and the children needed? What difference did any targeted intervention make, e.g. to address sibling conflict?

- If applicable, did their SDQ assessment of the child/ren accord with that of education staff? If there are significant differences in their assessment of a child, what might account for this disparity?

- What are the foster carers' views about placement together or apart? If you do not share their views, identify the reasons for this.

The observations of education professionals

Understanding each child's behaviour and presentation in different settings is an important component of the assessment. Staff in playgroups and other pre-school settings are likely to have a detailed knowledge of the child as well as how he or she relates to other children, similarly for teaching staff working with any school-aged children. There are two forms set out in Appendix 2, one for pre-school staff and another for use when children attend school. These can be adapted but provide a starting point for information that you might seek. Ideally, the form that you use should be sent electronically to each education setting so that they can email the completed document back to you. This information can then be included in your assessment report alongside any SDQ analysis based on SDQs completed by teachers. The SDQ may be sent to education staff but preferably should be completed during a school visit or a time set aside for a phone discussion.

The observations of health professionals

Health professionals often have considerable knowledge of children's early experiences within the family home and important information about how brothers and sisters were treated. Obtaining this can help you identify and evidence some patterns of interaction and how these might have begun, for example, perhaps the children's father favoured the boys in the family whilst daughters were treated less well. Health visitor records may provide a rich source of information about how each child was treated as well as their overall development. The sample letter set out in Appendix 2 can be used and/or adapted.

UNDERSTANDING NEEDS AND BEHAVIOURS – INCORPORATING SDQs INTO YOUR ASSESSMENT

When assessing placement options for each child, it will be important to have a good understanding of their individual needs. High levels of behavioural difficulties clearly have implications for what placements

ASSESSMENT: WHAT YOU SHOULD INCLUDE AND WHY

might be possible and might be more likely to be sustained over time (see Chapter 5). The SDQ can be a very helpful tool that contributes to your understanding of the children and their needs. This section sets out what is already required and how you might build on this within sibling assessments.

Since 2008/9, local authorities have been *required* to use the Strengths and Difficulties Questionnaire (Goodman, 1997) to collect information about children's emotional and behavioural health. Government guidance recommends that local authorities should use the SDQ to:

- inform a child's initial health assessment and health plan;
- identify specific emotional and behavioural difficulties that may warrant specific intervention; and
- help quantify the needs of the children in care to inform population-wide strategies for health services (Department for Education and Department of Health, 2015, pp10, 17, 30).

Completion of the SDQ is only required for children aged 4–16 who have been continuously looked after for a year.

The SDQ seeks information about 25 attributes grouped under five broad headings:

- Emotional symptoms (5 items)
- Conduct problems (5 items)
- Hyperactivity/inattention (5 items)
- Peer relationship problems (5 items)
- Prosocial behaviour (5 items)

When completed, 1 to 4 above are added together to generate a total difficulties score.

Slightly modified informant-rated versions exist for completion by parents and teachers. There is also a self-report version suitable for use with young people but this is less likely to be relevant for most sibling assessments. In general, SDQs completed by teachers are better at picking up on conduct problems (that is, more accurate reports) and parents/carers are better at noting emotional symptoms. Overall, SDQs are good at detecting conduct, hyperactivity, depressive and some anxiety disorders, but are poor at detecting specific phobias, separation anxiety and eating disorders. The SCIE expert working group (Milich *et al*, 2017, pp 27–28) also noted that:

> ....the Strengths and Difficulties Questionnaire (SDQ) alone is not an effective way to measure the mental health and emotional well-being of young people. Additionally, members advised that it is unable to detect

post-traumatic stress disorder (PTSD), attachment disorganisation and developmental issues such as autistic spectrum condition.

Government guidance (2013) suggests that if the SDQ completed by the carer results in a total difficulties score outside the normal range (i.e. a borderline score of 14–16 or a score of 17 or higher), then consideration should be given to a teacher completing an SDQ for the child and also the possibility of further mental health assessment.

Local authorities are likely to have issued their own guidance for completion in terms of DfE requirements. For versions of the SDQ and information on scoring and related aspects, see www.sdqinfo.com/.

DISCUSSION AND PRACTICE POINTS

Like any measure, the SDQ has limitations; however, used in conjunction with other means of assessment, and when findings are replicated across contexts (such as home and school), it can be very helpful. For example, it could help you to identify behaviours that are of concern and which are challenging for carers and/or education staff.

If the SDQ is used more flexibly than is required by the DfE, the results may assist you and help determine whether or not some additional intervention or assessment might be useful. Used early on, perhaps a month or two after entry into foster care, the SDQ can help you develop a baseline understanding of children's presenting needs – and subsequently if repeated, it can chart changes over time.

Consider using the SDQ for younger children, perhaps a slightly modified informant-rated version for the parents/carers or nursery teachers of two- (and four)-year-olds.* Again, this can help you to identify difficulties earlier on, for example, oppositionality in pre-school children.

SDQs – practice points to consider

- Use the SDQ earlier on after entry into care.
- Use with carers and education staff (pre-school and school).
- Use for children aged two–four, as well as for children over four years of age.

---

* As of June 2014, all SDQ questionnaires were relabelled to be consistent in giving '4–17 years' as the age range of the standard SDQ (i.e. 4–17 years, not 4–16 years) and giving '2–4 years' as the age range of the early years SDQ (i.e. 2–4 years, not 3/4 years). The content of the SDQs themselves is unchanged. The SDQs have been relabelled following evidence that the SDQ has good psychometric properties in two-year-olds, and that the performance of the SDQ in 17-year-olds is similar to that in 15- and 16-year-olds.

- Use the SDQ results to consider whether further intervention or assessment might be helpful.
- Set out the significant findings within sibling assessment reports.

ANALYSIS

An assessment needs to go beyond citing information and being descriptive to being analytical. 'The Anchor Principles: A framework for analytical thinking' (Brown *et al*, 2012) provides a helpful approach that can be used in a range of settings. Five questions are used to support analytical thinking; the framework has been tested by practitioners and has proved useful as a basis for both recognising and producing sound analytical assessments. When used sequentially, these five questions provide a framework for thinking that has become known as The Anchor because of its ability to anchor assessment firmly within the context of analysis. The five questions are:

1. **What is the assessment for?**

   This is vital in order to direct the assessment and ensure that you focus on the right issues.

   Within this section, practitioners may also begin to consider what existing knowledge they have that might be useful, keeping an open mind about how it might support their thinking from an early stage or lead to them reaching a different conclusion.

2. **What is the story?**

   This involves constructing a narrative that looks at the links between background history and current circumstances, incorporating the views of different family members and professionals. The authors note that:

   > *Different family members will often have different versions of the story and these may contradict each other. It's important that these different accounts and perspectives are woven into the narrative so they can be analysed and the contradictions understood and, when necessary, challenged or corrected. Telling the story requires us to think about what information is relevant, how different pieces of information relate to each other, and what this situation looks and feels like for those involved.*

   Within the context of a sibling assessment, it will, for example, be important to think about values and attitudes that might influence differential treatment of one or more children. Roles and expectations may be gendered, for example, boys may be more highly valued than girls or expected to be "tough". What might account for differences and gaps in relationships? For example, a caring maternal grandmother may have become ostracised from her grandchildren by a parent's controlling partner.

3. **What does the story mean?**

   This stage involves analysing and evaluating the information and reflecting on what this tells you about the needs of each child and the children as a group. The "documenting" needs to "show your working out" – that is, how the analysis led to and supports your conclusions. For example, a child's behaviour towards their siblings may be very different during contact with parents: what might this mean? The accounts of pre-school staff and the foster carer about some aspects of a child's presentation may vary significantly: what might account for this?

4. **What needs to happen?**

   The links made between the story, the meaning given to the story and what needs to happen (the plan) must be clear and logical. What placement/s are most likely to best meet the children's needs? What support and interventions might need to be put in place to promote children's development, including their identity needs? How might the pattern of contact need to change in order to help brothers and sisters develop and improve their relationship or to prepare for placement apart?

5. **How will we know we are making progress?**

   Having clear, measurable and specific outcomes that are linked directly to identified needs enables progress to be measured, and the plan to be adjusted if necessary. For example, family finding for a permanent placement for brothers and sisters to live together may be time-limited but it will be important to identify activities and key steps within the timeframe. Similarly, work may need to be done with each child before they are "ready" to move, whether this is with or without their siblings.

CIRCUMSTANCES THAT MAY INDICATE THAT SIBLINGS SHOULD BE PLACED SEPARATELY

There are a number of factors that may indicate the need for permanent separation. For example, very intense levels of conflict, and/or dominant or abusive patterns of behaviour may mean that placement together is not viable or is not best for some siblings within the group. Careful consideration needs to take place for siblings who have been sexually abused as to whether they can be placed together permanently. Specialist input may be required to fully understand and balance risks.

Gerrilyn Smith, a clinical psychologist, set out a number of circumstances indicating that siblings may need to be placed separately. These are based on her extensive clinical experience (personal communication quoted in Lord and Borthwick, 2008). Smith stated that if some children are placed in the same family, it may be impossible (within a reasonable timescale) to help them recover from dysfunctional and destructive patterns of interaction from the family of origin. These patterns include:

- *intense rivalry and jealousy, with each child totally preoccupied with, and unable to tolerate, the attention that their sibling/s may be getting;*

- *exploitation, often based on sex, e.g. boys may have been seen (in their birth family) and see themselves as inherently superior to their sisters, with a right to dominate and exploit them;*

- *chronic scapegoating of one child; maintaining unhelpful alliances in a sibling group and family of origin conflicts – sibling patterns of behaviour may be strongly entrenched and may prevent re-parenting or learning new cultural norms;*

- *maintaining unhelpful hierarchical positions, e.g. a child may be stuck in the role of victim or bully;*

- *highly sexualised behaviour with each other;*

- *acting as triggers to each other's traumatic material and potentially constantly re-traumatising each other. The triggers may well be unconscious, unintentional and mundane.*

It should be noted that any of the above patterns and ways of relating may be transferred by a child into his or her new family even if separated from birth siblings and placed singly. New parents need to be made fully aware of these patterns of interaction. Lord and Borthwick (2008, p22) identified other reasons that may make it very difficult or unwise to place some siblings together:

- *An older sibling may not be able to invest emotionally in a new family and will hinder the emotional investment of a younger child.*

- *There can be considerable age difference between siblings placed. Sometimes, the care plan for a much older sibling may be for permanent foster care with regular direct contact with birth family members but for a much younger sibling, adoption in a new family with indirect contact with the birth family is in their best interest.*

- *Sometimes a relative of one of the siblings offers a home to that child but not to others and this adult–child relationship is assessed as more important to the child than the sibling one.*

- *Sometimes a child may have a significant attachment to another carer and it is too damaging to disrupt this in order to unite or reunite the child with other siblings.*

- *Sometimes the size and age range of the group means that there are a very limited number of families available. After time-limited family finding, a sibling group may therefore need to be separated, but it is important that ongoing contact arrangements are made which can support the maintenance of their relationships.*

For factors that are implicated in higher levels of adoption breakdowns for children in sibling groups, see Chapter 10 and in particular the summary.

IDENTIFYING WHO SHOULD BE PLACED WITH WHOM AND CONSIDERING PERMANENCE OPTIONS

The level of need of individual children, the relationship between individual children, and their own wishes will all be important factors. Children separated in foster care may have been split by age – the younger ones together and the older ones in one or more placements. However, the experience of some adoptive families is that when children are very close in age, which they often are in large sibling groups, it can work best to consider placing children alternately, rather than in age order, i.e. the five- and three-year-old together and the four- and two-year-old together. This may work well if there is intense rivalry and competition, which can be greater between siblings who are very close in age, particularly if they are also of the same sex.

Separating children in permanent placement should only be contemplated following a full assessment of their needs, wishes and relationships, and this is likely to indicate who should be placed with whom, or whether they should be placed on their own. If the "ideal" is to place a large group together, efforts must be made first, albeit within agreed timescales, to recruit a family for the whole group. This is discussed in more detail in the next chapter. If children do have to be placed separately in this situation, and should family finding for the sibling group prove unsuccessful, the three key factors should again be:

- their individual needs;
- their wishes; and
- their relationships.

The same considerations are relevant to children who are very close in age, particularly if of the same sex, as discussed above. It will be essential to build in as much contact as possible for children separated because of a lack of resources. It will be important to try to recruit families who live fairly close to each other and who are committed to ongoing contact, involving the whole group for some weekends and holiday periods.

In considering the range of available **options to achieve permanence**, you will need to consider several dimensions rather than solely to focus on legal permanence. For example, what does permanence mean for a particular group of siblings and how can this best be achieved, taking into account their relationships with one another, their relationships with their current carers, and their relationships with the wider family? Would adoption of one or more of the children involve a severing of the child's sibling relationship or could meaningful contact be nurtured? What are the likely implications of a particular plan for the children during their childhood and into adulthood? Boddy (2013) conducted a thorough review of the evidence on permanency planning as part of the Care Inquiry. In her conclusion, she stressed the importance of taking account of children's wishes in permanency planning to promote their sense of belonging and the best possible care. She highlighted that 'what matters is quality and relationships'. Relationships were described as the "golden thread" that should be at the heart of all planning for children. The options for each child need to be considered in terms of: aiming to provide high quality and stable care; supporting children's sense of identity and belonging; and connecting past, present and future through childhood and transitions (2013, p5).

For some brothers and sisters, it may be far more important to keep them together than for some to be adopted and for others to remain in foster care with much reduced or no contact. The benefits and losses associated with different options will need to be balanced and often will need to be considered within a defined time period, for example, the search for an adoptive family for a large sibling group to stay together may be considered for several months or longer, but not indefinitely. The availability and quality of permanence options will inevitably have an impact on what choices are ultimately made.

MAKING DECISIONS

Local authorities are required to have a clear decision-making process that enables social workers to decide early on whether it is in the best interests of each child to be placed together or separately. Authorities must also consider the impact of the decision on each child (Children and Families Act 2014, Adoption and Care Planning (Miscellaneous Amendments) Regulations 2014, Regs 12A and 12B). The ways in which the assessment is conducted, who has been involved, and how the decision has been reached are all aspects that have ramifications for how explanations are subsequently given to and understood by children and their families. However, Dibben *et al* (2018, p16) have highlighted that decisions about placing children together or apart were not well evidenced, and in particular that there was an absence of reflective supervision, sibling assessment activity and recording of decision making.

An assessment that has included the observations and views of a range of professionals and family members, as well as the social worker, is likely to be perceived as "fairer" than a decision that predominantly stems from or appears to be based largely on the observations of one individual. Similarly, it is important to evidence how observations have been made over a period of time and also that they have occurred in a range of settings. The following two brief accounts outline different ways in which evidence may have been collated and how a "multi-sourced" and better evidenced account may assist decision-making. The issue described here relates to a brother's aggression towards his sisters:

> *Tommy, aged five, has shown aggressive behaviour towards his two sisters, Ellie (six) and Leah (three) since being placed with them in their current foster home. Evidence has been presented earlier on in this report that the children were exposed to a high level of recurrent domestic violence, mainly from their father towards their mother. The children's foster carer, Mrs M, says that Tommy has always behaved aggressively towards his sisters since the siblings were placed with her.*

Or:

> *As detailed already, Tommy P (aged five) and his sisters, Ellie (six) and Leah (three), were exposed to a high level of domestic violence for much of their early life prior to coming into care. Earlier in this report, observations by the health visitor, in particular, set out different and preferential treatment by the father towards Tommy including when this was first observed. The health visitor described how Tommy was allowed to choose what he wanted "first", and that if Ellie (and subsequently Leah) was playing with an item that Tommy took from her, then this was not addressed by either parent. The maternal grandmother, Mrs W, provided information about how Tommy was encouraged to be "tough", watched a lot of American wrestling programmes with his father, and that Tommy 'often hit Ellie' and also his mother. Mrs W also stated that this began when Tommy 'was just a toddler' and happened 'when Ellie annoyed him – for no obvious reason'.*

> *Since placement in foster care five months ago, Tommy has shown similar patterns of behaviour within parental contact as evidenced by extracts from contact observations set out already within this report. The accounts provided of past behaviour at pre-school and within school now have also raised a high level of concern about Tommy attempting to hit out and control others, particularly girls and female teaching staff.*

ASSESSMENT: WHAT YOU SHOULD INCLUDE AND WHY

The children have been placed with Mrs M for five months. She is an experienced foster carer who has provided placements for sibling groups for more than 10 years. Her detailed observations about the children provide additional information about their relationships with one another and in particular about how she has tried to address Tommy's aggressive behaviour. It is important to highlight that the foster carer has also been supported over the past three months to use strategies suggested by Ms S, a psychologist. As set out in the body of this assessment, my own work with and observations of the children are in line with these accounts. It is noteworthy that in individual work with her, when provided with a list of character traits to select using a tick or circle, Ellie ticked the following traits to describe her brother: mean, nasty, joker, noisy, horrible. She was able to give examples of some of Tommy's behaviour that supported her choices and when talking about this she started to cry. In another direct work session that focused on people whom she felt close to and others whom she got on less well with, Ellie placed the post-it note with Tommy's name on it furthest away from her own name and actually said 'I don't want it on here' (that is, she did not want his name on the large piece of paper).

RECORDING – THE IMPORTANCE OF CLEAR WRITTEN EXPLANATIONS FOR CHILDREN AND THEIR FAMILIES

For some children, the trauma of separation can be profound and the sense of loss may be longstanding. It is vitally important to record decisions and provide explanations to children as to why separation has occurred or will occur. This record should include:

- details of whose views and observations were sought (for example, family members; foster carers; health and education staff);

- the children's own views and the reasons, where and if applicable, why it was decided to override these;

- a summary of efforts that were made to keep the children together, if this had been the initial plan;

- the social worker's assessment outlining the main reasons for the plan and feelings associated with this (for example, *We really worked hard to....We felt sad when we couldn't find a foster family to look after you all together, We hoped that...*)

This written information should be given to the new family, included in each child's life story book and also be available on each child's adoption file held in the agency. When the children become adults, they may or may not feel that the right decision was made but they should at least be clear that it was made with thought and care, after a thorough assessment.

It is also helpful to think about the best ways of incorporating this significant information in later life letters for children. Providing a more limited explanation for children when they are very young can then be built on at key developmental stages when children and young people are likely to need and want more detail.

KEY PRACTICE POINTS

- It is crucial to conduct a full assessment of each child in a sibling group as well as an assessment of their relationships with one another. Children and their families should be actively involved in the assessment.

- Work needs to be planned so that there is enough time to gather important information, including from previous carers and from professionals in health and education settings. Planning should also allow for seeing children at different times and in different groupings or settings, dependent on their age.

- Assessments should make good use of background information and observations that have already been made but should also include up-to-date information. Patterns of behaviour that may have changed, as well as those which continue, should be identified.

- Say what you see: describe what you see and what others see (or have seen) – the assessment should include examples of both positive, pro-social behaviours as well as any concerns.

- SDQ assessments should be used for children aged three and older. Foster carers and, wherever possible, education staff should complete the SDQ.

- Significant observations should be corroborated using more than one informant or source so far as possible. Any significant differences in accounts should be addressed and reasons for them considered.

- Include relevant research, for example, findings from adoption outcome studies.

Chapter 6
Involving children, providing explanations and doing life story work

INTRODUCTION

Children and young people need to be involved and to feel involved. Evidence from research has highlighted that:

The degree to which children and young people are at the centre of assessment and decision-making in a meaningful manner, depends on the capacity of practitioners, supported by the systems in which they train and work, to form relationships and communicate effectively with them.

(Whincup, 2010, p1)

Being creative about how you engage with children about what may be difficult issues is not always easy but it is important to children in its own right and will help achieve better outcomes. Depending on their age and development, children may have different communication preferences, for instance:

- listening to or writing a story that features sibling themes;
- drawing pictures about family and family life;
- using a toy phone to communicate;
- using puppets and dolls;
- choosing photos that represent their views;
- talking face-to-face;
- completing multiple choice questions, ticking or circling preferences.

Think about what work you could undertake with children on an individual basis and what might be helpful to talk and think about with them as a group.

Principles and values

Direct work will be an important component of your assessment. The following principles and values are helpful in respect of work with looked after children generally:

- Children have a right to information about their past and about plans for their future. This should include material that seeks to explain the actions of social care staff and the courts but which also incorporates perspectives from the birth family.

- Direct work with children should take account of the child's individual needs and circumstances, for example, their background, age and understanding, as well as any special or additional needs arising from ethnicity, language, disability and/or preferred means of communication.

- Direct work with children should begin at the outset when a child becomes looked after rather than commencing at the point of preparation for permanence.

- Children are more likely to establish and maintain trust in their social worker when direct work sessions are planned regularly to provide explanations and information as well as to understand the child's views. In the absence of early and regular opportunities to ask questions and voice concerns, children are less likely to share any fears and anxieties with carers or staff.

- Children need accurate, age-appropriate information about shortcomings in their care and their family's role in this – without this, children may develop unrealistic fantasies and inappropriate attribution such as self-blame.

- Direct work with children that allows them to exercise appropriate choice and control can help to reduce children's feelings of anger and powerlessness. Many children who are subject to care and adoption proceedings have experienced very little control over what happens in their lives, and they have often been exposed to chaotic and inadequate standards of care as well as multiple changes in their environment. A significant number of children will continue to experience a high level of change either as a consequence of becoming looked after or whilst being looked after: placement changes; separation from siblings; and loss of contact with family members. Provide opportunities for children to exercise a realistic, manageable level of choice and control. Examples include the order in which they complete some "wishing and feelings" worksheets with you, and choosing from several options for "wind down time" activities at the end of a session.

- Communication with children is likely to be enhanced by using a flexible range of age-appropriate materials. Tangible means of recording children's views and perceptions not only allow for children to contribute and to check what has been conveyed but also provide an important means of validating feelings.

Guidance – consultation with children

The Department for Education publication, *Putting Care into Practice: Training programme for the revised legal framework for looked after children* (implemented on 1 April 2011), contained some helpful pointers with regard to consultation with children to ascertain their views. A summary of the main considerations is set out below:

- **Consultation duty: a statutory requirement**
  - *Wishes and feelings have to be sought before making a decision – that is, while the decision is still open and unmade.*
  - *Children have to be consulted on any decision that directly affects them – including plans, services, support, placement, contact with family, stopping any service or changing any placement.*
  - *Wishes and feelings have to be ascertained 'as far as is reasonably practicable' – this means ascertaining those wishes and feelings whenever that can reasonably be done.*
  - *Children's wishes and feelings have to be 'ascertained' – even when the child is not able to communicate in the usual ways.*

- **Ascertaining feelings**
  - *We have to discover a child's feelings, and give them 'due consideration', while also taking age and understanding into account.*
  - *UK law goes further than the United Nations Convention on the Rights of the Child (which does not cover feelings).*
  - *We must accept and consider feelings as they are – we cannot challenge them, ask a child to justify them, or reject them because we think they are irrational or immature.*
  - *We cannot ignore the child's feelings, even if they are very young or have insufficient understanding or express clear wishes, about a decision to be made.*
  - *A child's age cannot legally be taken into consideration without also considering understanding.*

- **Judge competence by ability to understand, not by chronological age**
  - *Does the child understand the question?*
  - *Does the child understand the main reasons behind it?*
  - *Does the child understand what the alternatives are?*
  - *Does the child understand what will happen if they decide one way?*

- *Does the child understand what will happen if they decide the other way?*
- *Can the child weigh the relevant things up for themselves?*
- *Can the child say (or otherwise communicate) what they want for themselves?*
- *Can the child keep to the same view rather than changing it according to what has last been said to them?*

- **Myths and reality – key points**
  - *You do not have to do exactly what a child wants. Respecting wishes and feelings does not mean agreeing with all of their views.*
  - *You can be creative and imaginative in finding ways to communicate with children.*
  - *Children cannot become responsible adults overnight – they need to learn and be supported.*
  - *It is a mistake to allow children to avoid playing a full part in decisions which affect them.*

Work with children and observing brothers' and sisters' interactions during play

Whatever tools and techniques you use in your work with children, it will be important to think about and find out about:

- who they regard as siblings – this may include non-related siblings in the foster home or adult half-siblings about whom the local authority may have limited knowledge;
- how each child describes their siblings – key words they use if verbal (think about multiple-choice and trigger sheets);
- roles – understanding how each child is seen by his or her siblings and within the wider family;
- how they react after separation and on being reunited;
- how a child responds when their sibling receives adult attention, is praised, checked or reprimanded;
- whether there are differences observed across settings (foster care, pre-school, contact, etc) and if so, what this might suggest;
- whether there are any significant differences between the children with regard to how they speak about and relate to parents/carers. What impact has this had or might it have in the future?

What you use in your work with children will depend on their age, understanding and preferences as well as techniques that you have found work well for you. The following are just some suggestions that can be used:

- play, drawing and interactive materials toolbox;

- rapport building – knowing what each child likes (favourite games, TV programmes, foods, etc), preferred modes of communication;

- games, activities that involve making and doing something together – observe whether children are able to co-operate, to take turns and share in an age-appropriate way. Examples might include: building a house using Lego; icing fairy cakes with several tubes of different coloured ready-made icing and sprinkles that they need to share; making a den together using cardboard boxes and other materials; spending time having a meal with children and noting how they might compete for food that needs to be shared between them such as a bowl of fruit, crisps or biscuits, a pack of different flavoured yogurts;

- listening to or writing a story that features sibling themes – involve children by asking questions such as: what do you think happens next? Observe children's emotional responses and capacity to attend, to be quiet and to listen for short periods of time;

- drawing pictures about family and family life;

- using a toy phone to communicate;

- using puppets and dolls;

- choosing photos that represent their views;

- choosing emoji faces to show how they feel (happy, sad, etc);

- circles and ecomaps.

Dolls' house or drawing the family home

This can help to focus on what happened in each room from the children's perspective. Who shared a bedroom? Use a selection of emoji faces to help children think about what elements may have been fun or made them feel happy as well as any aspects that they might not have liked.

Whom do you feel close to?

Use photos, a drawing or a name badge for each sibling and write down the names of each person in the foster family and any pets that the child may feel close to; also have available some blank cards or post-it notes. Ask the child with whom you are working to place their name or photo in the middle of a large piece of paper. Explain that the exercise is about whom they feel closest to, and show the child how they can place a name or photo right next to them if they love or get on really, really well with that person. If they don't like a person and have lots of fall-outs, then they can place that name or image at the very edge of the paper.

Use multiple choice and trigger statements that children can complete to express their feelings about a sibling or for other family members, for example:

The brother/sister/person I have most fun with is...

If I am feeling sad I can talk to...

If I need help I can ask...

When I want to play a game, I know X will usually play with me.

Your magic holiday island

Use a drawing of an island with two tents – one in the middle of the forest on the island and one by the beach. Help the child to think about who they would want to join them first of all on their island. Let them add names of additional people, one by one. Ask: *What would be good about having X on the island with you? What would you do together?*

Ask them which tent they would choose to sleep in and then find out who they would like to have sleep in the same tent.

Three houses exercise

Developed in New Zealand by Weld and Greening (2004), the Three Houses tool was originally designed to help workers include the voices of children and young people within child protection work. A simplified version is used to help workers understand children and young people's views about what is happening in their lives and to help children participate in the assessment and planning process.

- House of Vulnerabilities or Worries
- House of Strengths or Good Things
- House of Hopes and Dreams

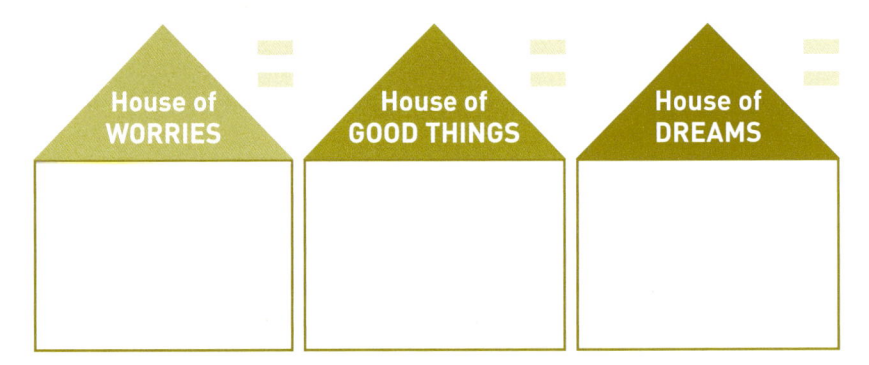

House of WORRIES

House of GOOD THINGS

House of DREAMS

See Weld and Parker, *Using the Three Houses Tool*: this resource booklet can be downloaded from the Partnering for Safety website at www.partneringforsafety.com. There is also a Three Houses DVD available on the site that demonstrates using the tool with a young person.

If you are working with children who have completed the Three Houses exercise, think about what they shared and how you might adapt the exercise to focus on their relationships with brothers and sisters, for example:

- House of Worries – me and Ashley
- House of Good Things – me and Selena
- House of Hopes and Dreams – me, Ashley and Selena

Lists of traits and words to describe brothers and sisters

Use lists of personal qualities and characteristics that a child can circle or tick from words that they associate with each sibling, such as: fun, quiet, kind, nice, nasty, cute, OK, happy, sad, thoughtful, joker. Check that words used are understood by the child. After they have ticked or circled characteristics, ask them to share examples or reasons for some of their choices. Include space at the bottom of the page for them to add other words that they can think of that describe their sibling. Young children may also relate to emoji faces that can be used similarly to show a few basic emotions.

Suzy, aged six, was asked to select words that she might use to describe each of her three siblings. She selected almost exclusively positive traits that she associated with her two younger siblings, Pippa, aged four, and Max, aged three – ticking words such as funny, cute and nice. She was able to provide some examples when prompted as to what had led her to tick these qualities. In the space beneath: *Add other words that you can think of that describe your sister Pippa*, she had asked me to write the word "joyful". In talking to her about this, it was very clear that Suzy understood the meaning of the word. She and her class had been doing work about Christmas being a happy and joyful time, and they had sung a Christmas carol where the word "joyful" was used. Suzy was also well able to describe to me some of the amusing things that her sister Pippa did that led Suzy to want to use this word. She told me that she and Pippa liked playing with dolls and giving each other "snuggle hugs". She was also able to provide supporting examples of why she thought that Pippa could 'sometimes be mean' – describing that sometimes Pippa did not want to play the games that Suzy did or that Pippa wanted to be the princess when she wanted this role herself.

In working with Suzy and thinking about her relationship with her older brother Jordan, aged seven, Suzy selected largely negative traits and was quick to complain about his behaviour towards her. She fought back tears as she shared some of the nasty things that he had done, both in the past whilst living with parents and more recently since placement in foster care. She expressed hurt that their father 'always' believed Jordan (and her other brother, Max), and conveyed that both parents treated her less well than they treated her brothers. Nonetheless, Pippa had enjoyed some aspects associated with 'taking care' of her younger brother and most especially her younger sister, and she had felt valued in this role.

Encouraging children to describe their experiences and to give examples is important as it provides valuable contextual information that will help you to gauge the significance of behaviour. A child may have argued and fought with their sibling earlier that day but this may quickly have been largely forgotten, or may be part of a more worrying and pervasive pattern of behaviour. A child's facial expression and body language when communicating about their siblings will also offer important clues about feelings.

As mentioned in an earlier chapter, a publication by Child Welfare Information Gateway (2013) suggests that workers should talk with children individually and ask age-appropriate questions, such as:

- Which sibling do you enjoy spending time with?
- Which sibling enjoys spending time with you?
- Who will play a game with you?
- Which sibling do you turn to when you are afraid or hurt?
- Which sibling turns to you when he or she is afraid or hurt?

Below is a list of some useful resources.

The SCIE online resource, *Using Play and the Creative Arts to Communicate with Children and Young People* (and e-learning and text resource) is available at: www.scie.org.uk/e-learning/communication-skills.

CoramBAAF also has a number of guides on direct work with children, in different settings, including communicating through play, different storytelling techniques, resilience-based activities, and a training pack on listening to children's wishes and feelings. These are all listed in Useful Resources.

EXPLANATIONS AND LIFE STORY WORK

It is important that work is undertaken with children so that they achieve a developmentally appropriate understanding of key decisions taken and plans made for them and their siblings. In the years ahead, children need to be able to develop a coherent narrative as they grow and their adopters will also need a good understanding and access to support.

Macaskill (2002, p140) highlighted how vital it was that children understood professional decisions about splitting them: if this work was not thoroughly addressed, unresolved issues were likely to adversely affect future contact between siblings.

Schofield and Beek (2018, p354–5) describe:

An attachment theory-informed approach to life story work would take as a starting point the child's need to have information that enables them to put together a coherent story, one that has meaning for the child, has a beginning, a middle, a here and now – and a sense of what the future might hold...Attachment theory would emphasise that what children need above all if they are able to reflect on themselves and present themselves to and communicate openly with others, is a coherent narrative that makes sense and which leaves them with a view of themselves and their history that can be reflected on without being overwhelmed or having to defend against thinking about the past. If children have to work so hard to exclude the past from conscious thought, it can limit their capacity to engage with and experience the world differently in the present.

The therapeutic value of good quality life story work and materials should not be underestimated. Selwyn (2017, p21) states that:

Life story work can be considered as a form of therapy and is about assimilating past events and the effect of significant people on a child's life.

However, many adoptive families have expressed concern with the quality of this work: Selwyn *et al* (2014) reported the views of 70 adopters where parenting had been very difficult or the placement had broken down. In that context, life story work and life story books were discussed in interviews. Adopters' accounts were generally negative, with concerns raised about the poor quality, incompleteness or inaccuracies of life story books and of the challenges of writing material that is suitable for children as they grow older. In some cases life story work was reported to be detrimental to children and as having a direct impact on the escalation of children's difficulties.

Adopters report variable quality of books and support provided by their agency to help them make best use of life story information (Watson *et al*, 2015; Hadley Centre and Coram Voice, 2015). In a recent study of adoptive parents' experiences (not specific to sibling adoption), the most frequently wanted service by adopters, and which they never received, was life story work (Neil *et al*, 2018).

Statutory guidance (DfE, 2013) specifically states that: 'All children with a plan for adoption must have a life story book' (para 3.10, p45). This guidance requires that life story books be given to the child and adoptive parents in stages, and the completed book presented within 10 working days of the adoption order. CoramBAAF produces a colourful workbook that can help children record memories and recollections; *My Life and Me* has space for drawings, photos, documents and more (see Useful Resources).

We should be clear about describing difficult events and decisions: as Dibben *et al* (2018, p15) recently wrote:

> *Adopted young people emphasised the need for quality life story work and information sharing. They wanted social workers to be unafraid of delivering the facts, concretely to them, at a young age, and developing this story as they progress through developmental milestones.*

Rees (2017) recommends using a *present – past – present – future*, approach as being more child-centred. She provides the following tips for compiling a life story book:

- It must be an honest account but "child-friendly" – social work jargon should be avoided.
- It should be appealing and colourful and contain scanned photos and clip-art.
- It can be divided into short sections so that it can be shared in "bite-sizes".
- It should engage the child by gently and playfully inviting him or her into their story.
- Writing in the third person is generally more appropriate for young children.
- Positive subliminal messages should be threaded throughout the story.
- It should be a celebration of the child's life and leave him or her with a sense of a positive future.

Guides on life story work with younger children, as well as one focusing on using digital media with adolescents, are available from CoramBAAF, as is a children's guide that explains what life story work is (see Useful Resources).

KEY PRACTICE POINTS

- Children and young people need to be involved and to feel involved. Being creative about how you engage with children about what may be difficult issues is not always easy but it is important to children in its own right and will help achieve better outcomes.

- Children are more likely to establish and maintain trust in their worker when direct work sessions are planned regularly to provide explanations and information as well as to understand the child's views.

- Think about what work you undertake with children on an individual basis and what might be helpful to talk about – and to think about – with them as a group.

- Depending on their age and development, children may have different communication preferences. It is important to be flexible and to offer some choice, and to try a range of ideas, tools and techniques in order to find out what works best for each child.

- Children need accurate, age-appropriate information about shortcomings in their care and their family's role in this – without this, children may develop unrealistic fantasies and inappropriate attribution such as self-blame.

- Children need help to understand what will happen in the future. This work is crucially important, as is the need for messages and explanations to be consistent so that brothers and sisters can be helped to develop a shared understanding.

- Explanations and accounts that are provided should strive to take account of changing needs over time. The questions that an eight- or 12-year-old may ask are likely to be rather different from those of a five-year-old. Life story materials should reflect this.

Chapter 7
Recruiting and preparing new families

INTRODUCTION

This chapter focuses on individuals and families as they embark on their adoption journey through to an overview of support issues that are especially pertinent to sibling adopters and their children. As in previous chapters, it is recommended that a child's relationships with siblings need to be embedded in adoption policy and practice at each stage. The experiences of families who have adopted brothers and sisters is drawn on and highlights some of the issues that are particularly important to get right.

Firstly, the needs of siblings should be discussed and addressed with all prospective adopters and foster carers. They may be applying to adopt a sibling group or a single child but have a child or children already in their family whose brother or sister the new child will become. They may already have several children and be applying to adopt another sibling group. The child or children placed with them may well have brothers or sisters placed elsewhere and will need help to understand why this is and to maintain some contact with them if possible. Even if the family is childless and the child to be placed currently has no siblings, brothers or sisters may be born subsequently and adoptive families need to be prepared to receive news of this and to be asked, possibly, to be considered as parents for the second child too. They may well have a clear wish to apply for a second child at a later date, thus creating a sibling pair.

RECRUITING PERMANENT NEW FAMILIES

There is considerable variation in practice in terms of children being placed with brothers and sisters: one study in the Adoption Research Initiative, *Family Finding and Matching: A survey of adoption agency practice in England and Wales*, Summary 4 (2011) found that the proportion of children placed with a sibling varied across agencies from 14 per cent to 80 per cent of all placed children.

Policy initiatives or their absence, the availability of resources, as well as individual attitudes and commitment are all likely to have an impact. Experience shows us that families *can* be found for large sibling groups. Groups of four, five, six and more children have been successfully placed for adoption. Being passionate about finding the "right" family for a child or children can make a massive difference. Having a positive focus on the importance of relationships between brothers and sisters and taking a "life-long" perspective are key elements to embed in agency practice. This does not mean that it will always be best to place a child with his or her siblings, but it does mean that these relationships need to be understood and valued.

The National Recruitment Forum (2013) publication, *Guidance Note on Improving Practice on the Placement of Siblings for Adoption*, suggests that adoption managers and workers consider a range of issues, and asks:

- *Do all your recruitment and training materials reflect the fact that half the children waiting for adoption need to be placed with their siblings? Do they reflect the benefits and rewards of adopting siblings, both for the children and the adopters, and the availability of support packages? Do you make use of positive messages from research in your recruitment and training materials?*

and

- *When placing siblings for adoption, are you proactive in identifying support packages, prior to matching, offering both practical and emotional support? This could involve short-term packages to relieve the initial impact of a sibling group placement, as well as realistic ongoing financial support where needed, and which can be reviewed to take account of the children's ongoing needs.*

The same document also suggests messages that could be incorporated in recruitment work, such as:

- *For most people, their relationships with their brothers and sisters are the longest lasting relationship they will have. Could you help to safeguard that for children awaiting adoption?*

- *Did you know almost half the children waiting for adoption need to be placed with their brothers and sisters?*

- *The majority of sibling groups are two children who want to stay together.*

- *Did you know that practical and financial help can be available? This could include help with buying a larger car, help with housework or furniture.*

- *Being placed with a brother or sister can help a child settle into a new family and have a positive sense of who they are.*

When recruiting families for siblings, the importance of good quality photos and film material featuring children should never be underestimated. Brothers' and sisters' profiles being shared through adoption consortia, within regional adoption agencies, exchange days and children having the opportunity to attend adoption activity days (AADs) together can all increase the chances of finding a suitable family or families for them.

Adoption activity days are now an established means of family finding for many agencies seeking adopters, particularly for those children who pose more of a challenge in terms of family finding. This includes brothers and sisters where the plan is for them to remain together. Bringing approved adopters and waiting children directly together in a safe, fun and supported environment has proven to be very successful for finding matches for siblings. For example, during the year 2016–17, 45 per cent of children matched via attending activity days were part of a sibling group. In previous years, a sibling group of five was able to be kept together and subsequently adopted through a link found at an activity day (email communication from Sally Beaumont, Coram).

Adoption activity days can provide a valuable means for brothers and sisters to be involved in their own family finding. Adopters are able to observe for themselves the children's relationship and their unique personalities, which the traditional paper profile is rarely able to bring alive. Importantly, many adopters subsequently widen their approval terms to consider more than one child and the activity day provides their social worker with good supporting evidence to enable siblings to be considered.

> *I took a sibling group of two children (boy and girl) along to an AAD – we had had little success prior to this and had previously profiled them in a publication. A couple attended and realised that the children whom they had seen in the same publication were attending. They spent a great deal of time with the children and expressed an interest in them. The adopters subsequently read the CPR, a visit proceeded, and they are booked into panel for a match.*
>
> (Family-finding social worker)

It is important for local authorities to be as clear as possible at the recruitment stage about any support package that will be available. This applies whether publicity is focused on general recruitment or for a specific sibling group. Potential adopters of large sibling groups may be put off altogether if they think that support is not likely to be available.

Adoption of more than one child will be impossible for some families unless they receive practical and financial help. Individuals and families may choose to apply to an agency that "looks" as though it takes post-placement support seriously, or more seriously, than one that does not.

Agency websites have the power to influence early choices that prospective adopters make. Ensuring that these "feel" welcoming, accessible and present information in a lively way can make a huge difference. Experiential elements that share stories and engage "hearts and minds" is an important first step in connecting with potential adopters.

Helpful resources and reading

National Recruitment Forum (2013) *Guidance Note on Improving Practice on the Placement of Siblings for Adoption*, available at: www.first4adoption.org.uk/wp-content/uploads/2014/06/NRF-Sibling-Guidance-Notes.pdf

A presentation is also available at: www.first4adoption.org.uk/wp-content/uploads/2014/06/NRF-Presentation-of-Siblings-Checklist.pdf

Argent H (2008) *Ten Top Tips on Placing Siblings*, 'Tip 6: Recruit and prepare families for each sibling group'

Cousins J (2008) *Ten Top Tips on Finding Families* contains useful ideas and tips on recruiting families.

DWF Adoption (undated) *Peter, Stewart and Family*, video, available at: www.dfw.org.uk/how-adoption-works/watch-our-adoption-video

The video shows the story of a sibling group who were all adopted together because the adoptive parents believed that this was right and advocated for this to happen.

PREPARING, ASSESSING AND APPROVING FAMILIES

The vast majority of families who adopt siblings are childless and are motivated to keep brothers and sisters together. However, they also face many challenges, which are explored later in this chapter.

The beliefs and views of the social workers meeting applicants and conducting assessments are inevitably factors that can and do have an impact: they can influence decisions about whether siblings are placed together or separately and whether families are approved for large sibling groups or not. Some families, who are successfully parenting siblings, have shared their experience of having had to convince social workers, who tended to question how anyone could manage to take on more than two children at a time, of their capacity to consider a sibling group (for example, the video by DFW Adoption mentioned above).

In a helpful case study, Carden (2015) outlined her work on preparing, assessing and supporting adopters for a sibling group of five children aged from three to nine years. The children had a background of neglect and exposure to domestic violence prior to being placed in two separate foster homes. Carden highlighted that it would have been easy to become overwhelmed by these aspects rather than to focus on the children presenting as a close group who had supported each other. Assessment work with the children included using the Strengths and Difficulties Questionnaire (SDQ) and reviewing the impact of each child on their current carers as well as other elements. The importance of getting to know each child is emphasised. The account includes a detailed overview of support put in place to help the children and the family.

In a recent report of research by Coram Cambridgeshire, Dibben *et al* (2018, p11), noted that those who were considering adopting brothers and sisters wanted to see professional and financial support as well as additional training in place to help them, in particular:

> *More specific training on siblings at an early stage in the process could be helpful for both those considering and not considering siblings to further inform their decision-making, providing information about the rewards, challenges and support available. There is also value in using experienced adopters of siblings to talk to prospective carers which for some may be more influential than hearing from professionals.*

Prospective parents may approach an agency with a very clear idea of exactly how many children they want to consider, but other families have said that when social workers shared information about waiting children, the particular personalities and needs of children or a group of siblings struck a chord with them. All families need to know about the children who are waiting and it is often useful to cover this with individual families during the preparation process when more detail can be added.

Families often say that they learn most from talking with other families so it is useful to have easy access to your own sibling-adopter families locally and within your region. The experiences of sibling adopters should be incorporated at each stage: information, preparation groups, assessment, and support. Adoption UK offers a useful service to its members through its Experience Resource Bank of families with particular experiences: through this, applicants can be put in touch with parents who have adopted groups of brothers and sisters, and can benefit from their experience by talking on the phone and meeting.

The experience of one family is drawn on throughout this chapter to highlight some key issues.

Suzanne and Daniel adopted a sibling group of four children. As well as being adoptive parents, they both have extensive experience as child care social workers. Their children are:

Jack, aged 9
George, aged 8
Tom, aged 7
Mia, aged 5

The boys were placed almost five years ago and their daughter joined them six months later.

Motivation for adopting siblings

Daniel and I met and started our relationship whilst doing social work training. One of our first conversations was about children and we spoke about adoption at this time. The important thing for us was to become parents in the future and we both liked the idea of having a large family.

After we qualified, we both worked with children in the care of the local authority. Something that was really hard during this time was seeing the number of siblings who had to be separated when they were taken into care. The hardest one to deal with was when it was purely because they were a large family and there just wasn't a foster placement that could care for them all (our four children had three separate foster placements between them).

Our decision to adopt a sibling group of four came from our desire to have a large family. We also felt that we could offer our children the opportunity to stay together and grow together. We knew that if any of them were placed anywhere else we could not guarantee that they would even continue to see one another and even if they did it would not be enough for them.

Assessment – what helped prepare you? What was missing or might have been helpful?

Helpful: *Meeting the foster carers and learning about the children was helpful. At the start of our assessment our worker had identified a potential family for us and so we did a child-specific assessment. This was good as it allowed us to get our heads around the children and to start to get to know them well before we met them.*

It was great to do the training days where we got to meet other potential adopters. They were very useful days but we could have done with more of them, as it was a lot to cram into just four days.

Not helpful: *Our preparation and assessment focused on children and their attachments – we didn't get help to understand that attachment works both ways.*

A full financial assessment was not done with us prior to the children moving in and we were reassured that it would all be OK and it would get sorted. Realistically, we knew, as did those assessing us, that Suzanne would not be able to return to her full-time post once we had the children and we talked about it but we were not supported to put in a plan. We then had to fight with the local authority to get the adoption allowance sorted.

Things that would be good to have known – or to have known more about

Suzanne: Attachment works both ways. When we adopted our four children, I had never considered how I would attach to them, which now seems crazy as I had a lot of experience of working with children. I had thought that it would happen instantly and naturally, but it didn't for me and I felt terrible. I also didn't tell anyone this as I felt really guilty as I had wanted to be a mum for so long. I remember going into one of my son's bedrooms initially, and it didn't smell of our house, it smelt very floral like the foster carers' house. This was reassuring for him but felt very strange for me.

Understandably, I felt quite strange suddenly going from being a couple to a large family. I had feelings that I recognised to be similar to post-natal depression and looked up if there was such thing as post-adoption depression. I knew a woman through work who had set up a charity for families who suffered post-natal depression and I found her help vital initially; I never attended a group but I did follow her group on social media and I also had contact with her via private messaging. I put so much pressure on myself to be the perfect mother, especially because our children had suffered trauma and needed better than "good". I could never live up to my own expectations and I have had to work hard to overcome the feelings of guilt and not being good enough.

KEY ASPECTS TO EXPLORE AND ADDRESS IN ADOPTION ASSESSMENTS

- The applicants' own experience of siblings, both the sibling group, if any, in which they grew up and also sibling relationships that they know of through their family and friendship networks. How might these experiences influence them and what might be different for brothers and sisters placed for adoption from care?

- The possible impact of adversity on children's relationships with siblings – including the impact of domestic violence.

- Understanding how emotional dysregulation may impact on children's relationships with siblings and peers.

- Understanding how children's emotional dysregulation may impact on adopters.

- Families need to be prepared for the fact that many siblings to be placed as a group are living in separate foster families and may have limited experience or even no experience of living together. On the other hand, some sibling groups may have very close bonds, which could feel quite excluding to new parents.

- Strategies for managing sibling rivalry and conflict. For example, the potential benefits of emphasising that each child is unique rather than being driven by children's relentless demands to be treated "equally".

- Managing differences between the children: different views, recall and experiences within their birth family; different levels of ability; different ways of managing emotions and communicating needs.

- Family time – interacting with the children together and also meeting individual needs.

- What the prospective parents' work day and weekend day look like now – how this might change if brothers and sisters are placed.

- Considering how they might feel differently about each child within a sibling group and how this might shift and change over time.

- Opportunities to talk to and meet experienced adopters of siblings, followed by discussion about what this contributed to their own thinking and learning.

- Considering contact with brothers and sisters placed elsewhere – sharing a range of adopters' experiences, learning about what helps and hinders sibling contact. Taking a long-term view – brothers and sisters through childhood into adulthood.

- Challenges and rewards – sharing a range of adopters' experiences. Emotional warmth may co-exist with high conflict so relationships may be mixed. Children may play well together and keep each other entertained and occupied or there may be lots of fall-outs. Brothers and sisters have a shared history – they can support each other and help each other remember what happened at home but this can also be difficult if their views and needs aren't similar or don't converge at certain times.

- Support: in particular, consider domestic chores; breaks; day respite with family and friends.

- Considering the effects of adopting a sibling group on a couple's own relationship.

THE IMPACT ON EXISTING CHILDREN

If the prospective adopters already have children, it is clearly important for them to be fully involved in the preparation process. Research (Rushton *et al*, 2001) indicates that the experience of being a sibling already may be useful preparation. However, even adult children who have left home can still experience jealousy and need to be carefully involved in the initial preparation. It is important to remember that incoming children may bring dysfunctional patterns of relating and behaving into the new family. Children already in the family are likely to be affected by this in some way. A child who has been separated from siblings and placed singly may also attempt to relate to any new children in the family as he or she did with birth siblings, e.g. taking on the scapegoat or victim role or attempting to bully or dominate. In their study of adoptive families in Wales, Meakings *et al* (2016) found that families that already had a child or children experienced the adoption process as being focused almost exclusively on the adopted children, at the expense of other children in the family. Based on their findings, the authors stressed that:

The decision to keep together, separate or create sibling relationships through adoption should be viewed as the start of a process of family formation, reformation or consolidation, and one which requires ongoing support for all siblings and the adopted family.

SUPPORT WITHIN THE ADOPTERS' NETWORK AND BEYOND

Support after placement will be essential, and is discussed in more detail in Chapter 11. Agencies need to explore with families during the assessment and preparation stage what their own support networks will be and also to be clear about what support the agency will be able to offer. It is important for new parents to be able to spend some time with each child individually and they will need to think about how they will manage this.

TRAINING, PREPARATION AND THE ADOPTION PANEL

Adoption agencies should consider how best to include specific elements that address the needs of siblings and adopters. Within this guide there is reference to many research studies. This bank of research clearly demonstrates that much more needs to be done to help prepare and support adoptive families. This is the case whether they are parenting a sibling group of two or more, or are managing contact between brothers and sisters. Some agencies have already begun to develop their services. Collaboration, including regional initiatives, may provide further impetus to sharing best practice and enhance the capacity for innovation.

Adoption panel members may also benefit from additional training as well as an understanding of agency preparation. Panel members can sometimes be cautious about approving applicants, particularly childless people, for more than two children. Each individual and family is unique and their application should be considered carefully on its own merits. It is important that panel members are aware that childless applicants, and those with children, have successfully adopted large sibling groups of four or more children. Families who attend the panel to present themselves and answer questions directly may feel more confident that they have been able to fully address these, and other, aspects.

Whilst much work will be done prior to approval, subsequent preparation and training to help families get ready for a particular sibling group are equally important. Many families tell us that they are more able to absorb and make sense of information that relates to individual children with their own unique personalities and histories.

The Coram Cambridgeshire Think Siblings project (Dibben *et al*, 2018) has developed modules that can be used to help prepare and assess prospective adopters.

- Stage 1: e-learning materials for prospective adopters.
- Stage 2: post-approval training for prospective adopters.
- Post-placement workshops for adopters of children in a sibling group.

For more information, visit: www.coram.org.uk/thinksiblings.

KEY PRACTICE POINTS

- Siblings and their particular needs should be included in recruitment materials and be considered with all prospective carers and adopters. Most families will be affected in some way. Relationships between brothers and sisters may be supported through placement together or by contact if they are separated. Other sibling-like relationships may be created by living together in foster care or legally through adoption.

- Prospective adopters and parents often say that they learn most from talking with other families. The experiences of sibling adopters should be incorporated at each stage: information; preparation groups; assessment; and support. Similarly, the voices of children and young people who can share their experiences of being separated or kept together with siblings can have a powerful impact.

- Whilst much work will be done prior to approval, subsequent preparation and training to help families get ready for a particular sibling group are equally important.
- Families tell us that they need more support to help promote better relationships between brothers and sisters – whether or not these relationships began in their birth family or many years later.

Chapter 8
Preparing to move, matching and introductions

INTRODUCTION

About 60 per cent of children waiting to be adopted need to be placed with one or more of their siblings. There is a particular shortage of adoptive families offering to adopt more than two children. In a review of adoption research studies, Thomas (2012, p44) noted that:

Delays in widening searches and a lack of realism about the prospects of finding suitable families for particular children were the main issues that hindered family finding. Children's social workers sometimes strove to find a notional "ideal" family for children, and were unwilling to alter requirements; for instance, when there was an insistence on a two-parent adoptive family, or placing a large sibling group together even when no family could be found.

It is important to remember that:

- a detailed, up-to-date assessment should be used to inform the matching process;

- children's needs or difficulties should not be under-played;

- whoever instigates the match, getting a good "fit" between adopters' preferences and children's needs will help promote placement quality and stability;

- criteria that exclude or may "put off" adopters should not be used unless there are clear, well-evidenced reasons to do so.

SHARING INFORMATION

An important building block when planning placements is the quality and depth of information that is shared. Detailed, well-presented information that brings the children's needs and personalities alive will not only help adopters to make informed choices but will also mean that they are better prepared to meet children's needs. Selwyn *et al* (2014) found that more than two-thirds of adopters felt that important information had not been shared or fully explained. Gaps in information provided may engender feelings of distrust in staff and make it harder for parents to respond with understanding and sensitivity to cues from children. Thomas (2012, p41) identified that:

> *There was some evidence of inadequate information sharing about the children's emotional and behavioural difficulties in the finding a family processes. Consequently, some adoptive parents found that the children placed with them had more profound difficulties than anticipated.*

The written views and observations of foster carers should have been obtained as part of the sibling assessment (see Chapter 5) and this document, alongside others, will be central to early discussions with the adoptive family or families. All observations need to be placed in context: there may be differing views about placement between foster carers looking after a split sibling group; education staff and others may also have expressed views about placement together or apart. The challenge for the social worker is how to ensure that they pull all the information together. Presenting a coherent analysis of how and why decisions were made is crucial as this will help adopters to understand and appreciate the complexity of what has gone before.

An open dialogue within which adopters are encouraged to ask questions about decision-making will help. Their understanding is likely to be linked with increased emotional acceptance and empathy – without this, it will be even harder for them to help children integrate difficult aspects of their past. The concept of developing a coherent narrative can helpfully be used to think about the journey on which adopters are embarking as well as for children as they develop and, in years ahead, ask questions about what happened and why. Neil's research over many years has highlighted the significance of empathy and adopter communicative openness, exploring how this links not only with birth family contact but also with adopted people having a more cohesive sense of identity (see www.uea.ac.uk/contact-after-adoption).

Adopters should be able to see and comment on the provisional text of their prospective child/ren's life story materials. This can help adopters not only to understand how past events and decisions have been conveyed but also provides an important opportunity for them to make suggestions. It will be especially important that clear explanations about placement plans are included in each child's materials and that these are consistent. It is helpful to think about providing life story material in stages – for example, a basic version for a four-year-old at the current time can be supplemented by additional material and "questions and answers" to be given and talked through several years later.

Families that have experienced them generally report that they very much valued a child appreciation day or life appreciation day being held before introductions start. This can provide adopters with rich opportunities to ask questions of others who know or knew their children and offers a lively way of learning more about children's lives. Argent (2008, p19) stated that such days should be regarded as essential when placing siblings:

> *There is no better way for sharing a great deal of information in a relatively short time than to give over a whole day for prospective permanent carers to meet all the people who can contribute to an understanding of the siblings. It is a small investment compared to the cost of a disruption due to incomplete or misunderstood information. This is an opportunity for seeing and hearing a multi-faceted view of each child illustrated by videos, photos, anecdotes and facts, and of getting an impression of the impact the siblings have made on previous carers. The agency's legal, medical and educational advisers should be available for at least part of the day to clarify matters regarding the children's health, schooling and status in order to avoid misunderstandings and misinterpretations. Social workers can produce visual aids on flip charts: flow diagrams, family trees and circles to represent moves, losses, separations and relationships can sometimes communicate more than words. Such a day should be regarded as a guided tour through the children's lives: as one adoptive mother said, 'It gave us the chance to put the questions we didn't know we wanted to ask'.*

These meetings need careful preparation and good facilitation and they complement rather than take the place of individual meetings and written information. However, they can give a very rich, full and "living" picture of children. Thinking about how key information that is shared on the day will be recorded is important so this should be planned and provided in a timely manner.

CoramBAAF's guide, *Child Appreciation Days*, gives information on how to organise, prepare and run a Child Appreciation Day and includes a range of useful tools for those organising such events (see Useful Resources).

INTRODUCTIONS – PAYING ATTENTION TO CHILDREN'S AND ADULTS' EMOTIONAL NEEDS

Introductions are a busy and exhausting time often riven with many practical considerations, but fundamentally the primary focus must be on building relationships and managing complex emotions. Getting off to a good start really matters – not just in the short term but it can also have a longer reach. "Messages" conveyed to children at this point may affect whether children feel that they have permission to move, whether or not it feels emotionally safe, or whether it feels "disloyal" to their foster carers to move on.

It will be important to ensure that materials prepared by the adopters are accessible to all children in a way that is appropriate for their developmental needs. For example, an "About Us" family book prepared by the adopters may be needed for each child rather than only one copy being available; similarly in respect of photos and filmed material, especially if siblings are not all placed together in the same foster home but the plan is to reunite them. Careful attention paid to these initial stages will reap dividends during introductions and later on.

You could also use CoramBAAF's *Me and My Family*, a colourful and fun 'Welcome to our Family' book, through which adopters can introduce themselves to the child who will be joining them as well as for the child to work through and record the changes in their life as they move to their new family (see Useful Resources).

Boswell and Cudmore (2014) wrote about the complexity of children's feelings when they are being moved. They set out how, when faced with separation or loss, children sometimes withdraw into a compliant state. It can be hard for the adults around them to remain open to what is happening for them at a deeper level. We may believe, or want to believe, that a compliant or withdrawn child is genuinely "fine". Boswell and Cudmore remind us that this "blind spot" is particularly prevalent where adults themselves are dealing with huge amounts of stress and anxiety. They set up a website following their article (www.thechildrenwerefine.co.uk) and work with others to promote sensitive practice during transitions.

Their guiding principles focus on the child's attachment needs:

- the child's relationship with their foster carer should be maintained throughout the transition and beyond;
- the relationship between foster carer and adopter is a long-term commitment and needs to be supported and sustained;
- foster carers and their families need support and training during and after transition;
- adopters should be given training and support on understanding attachment and loss, not just before but after the move;
- training should be provided on recognising and responding to unspoken or latent feelings in a young child who appears to be "fine".

Neil *et al* (2018) found that poorly managed transitions were linked to poorer outcomes for children. In their study, about three-quarters of adopters felt well supported by foster carers during introductions and were happy with the quality of care that their child had received whilst placed with foster carers. Positive practice on the part of foster carers (Neil *et al*, 2018, pp77–78) included:

- being welcoming, friendly and encouraging;
- being open about information on the child, their routines, likes/dislikes etc; and
- preparing the child in advance by giving them information about their new family.

Conversely, difficulties identified by adoptive parents included:

- foster carers finding it hard to cope with loss or being possessive and controlling;
- foster carers not agreeing with the match;
- foster carers deviating from the plan (although flexibility was welcomed if the plan was not working);
- abrupt and poorly handled endings (for example, due to foster carers' painful feelings), which were upsetting for some children.

As Neil *et al* (2018, p110) summarised:

> *Those children who experienced the move to adopters as difficult were more likely to have poorer outcomes, when all other factors were taken into account…Children who are older at placement and who have experienced more maltreatment may be more at risk of a difficult transition – and these underlying factors may link to poor outcomes. However, in this analysis these other factors are held constant, suggesting that a distressing transition may in itself be a risk factor for children's later development.*

The Moving to Adoption Project (Beek, Neil and Schofield, UEA) piloted a practice programme with two local authorities on transitions from foster care to adoption. The project drew on theory, research and existing good practice and was underpinned by the Secure Base model (see www.uea.ac.uk/providingasecurebase/the-secure-base-model). A practice guide was subsequently developed (Neil *et al*, 2020). Guides for social workers and carers describing the Secure Base model, by Gillian Schofield and Mary Beek, and how to apply it are also available from CoramBAAF (see Useful Resources).

There is a detailed discussion of the issues that need to be considered when linking and introducing siblings in *Ten Top Tips on Placing Siblings* (Argent, 2008)

ADOPTERS AND FOSTER CARERS – THEIR RELATIONSHIP AND NEEDS

Children's readiness to engage with their new family and their capacity to move on will be crucially determined by the preparation undertaken by their social worker and foster family. There are often many practical considerations and constraints that may affect foster carers' availability and capacity to welcome adopters into their home. All introductions need to be carefully planned to take account of commitments that the foster carers have, including work as well as other considerations such as holidays, their own family, health and the needs of other children for whom they may be responsible. Too many competing demands can make it hard for foster carers to do all that they want to do to help adopters and children as they take their first steps to becoming a family.

The emotional readiness of foster carers as well as adopters is key. Understandably, some foster carers may struggle with their own feelings and in other instances the quality of care that they have provided may have been ambivalent or poor. Research by Selwyn *et al* (2014) highlighted the crucial importance of carefully managed and supported transitions. Difficulties during introductions were linked with higher rates of placement difficulties and breakdown. Nearly one-third of adoptive parents reported feeling unsupported and under strain during the introductions, whilst two-fifths of parents had misgivings about the quality of care provided to their children while in foster care. Poorly managed introductions and transitions were statistically associated with adoption disruption. The majority (61%) of adoptive parents spoke positively about the assistance provided by foster carers during the introductions to their children, but nearly one-third described foster carers as unhelpful or obstructive. For some of the foster carers, there had been unresolved feelings that impacted on their capacity to help children move on: carers who had wanted to keep the child themselves or had struggled with their own feelings of loss and grief. In these situations, children moved to their adoptive family without having been given "psychological permission" by foster carers to make new close relationships. Other children arrived in their adoptive families with very few, if any, personal possessions or toys. As the authors stated, these circumstances are likely to leave children feeling insecure and without a sense of who they are.

Adopters tend to feel better prepared for adoption in general terms but less well prepared for the particular child or children. Specific assessments can help when there is a possible match between prospective parents and a waiting sibling group. Foster carers have a vital role alongside children's social workers, as they help children prepare for moving. Whether or not the adults feel "comfortable" with each other will partly depend on the time that they have had to think about their own needs as well as those of others involved.

It is important to allow time for the foster carer to talk about their feelings to their supervising social worker and the child's social worker. Whilst fostering may be viewed as a "job", carers need to be able to talk about their feelings of loss. As one foster carer said:

> *We have given 24/7 care to these children and they feel like family. If we have time to talk about loss before adoption introductions begin, we will cope much better as the adoption moves forward.*

Foster carers' tips and ideas

Several experienced foster carers who have helped move brothers and sisters to adoptive families have shared the following tips and ideas (personal communication):

- Try to build a relationship with adopters before they meet the children. I would always use email and from the date of the matching meeting would send a short account of what the children had done that day and include pictures. In the following days, I send pictures that show how the children have expressed themselves – happy, sad, confused, cross – so the adopters can start to get to know their children before meeting them. When communicating with the adoptive family, I use the words "your children" and "your child".

- I often encourage children to make a banner with their names on and the names they are calling their new family so when the adopters come the children have something to show and share. This helps to give a focus, something to talk about, and starts building connections. I also try to take a photo of everybody holding the banner to start building memories for times ahead.

- Adopters are coming into your home so welcome them! A meal set up for the children and adopters together is a must – try and find a time when they come back after your family have eaten or take your family out leaving a meal for them to share. If children are old enough, they will delight in showing their adopters where mugs, plates and cutlery are kept, it will feel familiar for them.

- I listen to words from my foster children, when they start saying: 'What time is X coming?', when they start owning the adults: 'My mum says....' Little ones who are pre-verbal will give clues as to comfort-seeking by putting arms out, smiling, falling asleep when cuddled, being cuddled, climbing up onto a lap.

- Help very young children by using stickers on wall calendars for when introductions are happening. Have photos of the adoptive parent/s displayed in key places, e.g. the fridge door. When you have taken a photo of the children with the adopters, ask the children where to put this, outlining a few choices. Explain that you can print off several copies in case they each want a copy in their bedroom/s.

- Engage children in some of the information that you have shared or will be sharing with adoptive parents. For example, ask them about what they think is important to share. Use everyday opportunities, such as mealtimes, to talk about this: 'Let's write down that Ali likes porridge for breakfast and that you like toast and a banana – and that you both love a drink of milk'.

- Bath and bed times are sensitive times for children and attachment-building. Think carefully about how and when to involve adopters and make sure children are ready for this. Some things that might seem small really matter to children, like how you shampoo a child's hair so that they don't become upset or feel out of control.

- Remember to be really clear when sharing information about toileting, for example: 'Sam likes to be grown up and says he can wipe his own bottom. He tries really hard but his pants are often a bit smeared. This is getting better and I sometimes show him a clean pair of his used pants and praise him for doing such a good job'. And: 'Tyrone needs lots of fruit, vegetables and water every day to help keep his bowel movements regular. In the past he would sometimes say that doing a pooh hurt his bottom and I think he "put off" going to the loo. We make sure that he has time to sit on the loo after he has had breakfast, this seems to work well for him. It's important that he doesn't feel rushed or he will say that he doesn't need to use the toilet.'

- Don't be afraid to be really clear about how much information you share, however small. We have often said to adopters: 'Look, we might have gone a bit over the top here, but we'd rather share whatever we think might be of some help, however small.' In our experience, adopters have really appreciated this.

- Talk about the roles that children had when they first came to you. Although an older brother or sister might have stopped much of their "parenting" of younger ones, this may well surface again – especially if the children feel insecure.

- Think about how long it took for each child to show you affection and start to trust you. Some adopters seem to think that we are "super" foster carers and might imagine that the children liked us from the outset – we try and put them straight! Letting them know that it took time and that we're still learning is always good to share.

Learning from adopters

Suzanne and Daniel were specifically assessed as adoptive parents for three brothers who were initially placed five years ago; six months later, their little sister joined the family. As well as being adoptive parents, they both have extensive experience as child care social workers. Their children are now aged between five and nine years:

Jack, aged 9
George, aged 8
Tom, aged 7
Mia, aged 5

Introductions: what worked well? what was missing or might have been helpful?

Suzanne recalled:

I remember the first day that we met our boys, we saw these three little faces staring out at us from a climbing frame. We met them all at the same time which was great. It was overwhelming and they called us Mummy and Daddy straight away. I recall my husband saying to me how odd this felt as he did not feel that we had earned it initially. The day that we met is one of the boys' favourite stories and they often ask us to tell the story of how we met and like to chip in with what they did/said. We never got any photos of us meeting the kids. It would have been nice to have that very first sighting of one another, we didn't think to ask for it as we were so overwhelmed at meeting them.

Our introductions lasted for 10 days and were a mixture of the three boys together and we also spent time alone with our eldest and time with the younger two boys together. During this time the boys seemed to get on well together and really just enjoyed being with one another. George looked up to Jack and would copy him in how he spoke and when they played. I do not remember them competing for attention early on. They were little bundles of energy and we spent lots of time in parks in those 10 days and since then!

We were aware that questions had been raised about how Jack may attach with me and during introductions he was very focused on my husband. However, something about George concerned me more when I met him and I shared this with my husband. One of the things that worried me was that he did not appear to have any boundaries with unknown people.

The introductions were exhausting but the foster carers made us feel very welcome in their homes and fed us some lovely food! They were great at letting us get fully involved with the kids and shared lots of information with us. They provided photos of the children from their time in their homes and we love to share these now. We have also kept in touch with the foster carers and have been to visit them all.

Daniel and I would go home in the evenings shattered but made sure that we made the most of our last few days as a couple. The boys appeared to be very eager and ready to accept us as their parents. At times, I felt completely overwhelmed and unsure how we would cope. This feeling continued throughout the introductions and continued after we became a family. No one had spoken with us about feelings that may occur for us and I was worried about people thinking that I wasn't coping or that I wasn't good enough. There were lots of giggles and happy times alongside these feelings.

Moving in day *was very emotional for everyone concerned, it was hard on the children and the foster families. I felt like it should be a very exciting time but I was also conscious that we were taking them from somewhere that they had been happy and settled with people who really cared for them.*

It helped that we had taken most of the children's belongings before moving day and so there wasn't much to collect other than our three little men and we could just focus on them.

The children came with photos that were so important to them and to us and we love to look at these now. The rest of the day is a bit of a blur now and the next thing that I remember was when we had put them into bed. Daniel and I just sat and looked at one another and could not believe that we were suddenly parents to these three little boys who were upstairs in bed. It felt so scary and responsible. There was so much for us all to learn about one another.

The first day that my husband Daniel went back to work was the hardest. I felt outnumbered and like my life would never be the same again (it wouldn't be and will never be but that's OK now). Daniel returned to some level of normality but luckily I had family around to support me during that first week.

Soon after, the boys' baby sister Mia, aged six months, was introduced.

Suzanne wrote: *Once we had got through those early weeks, we were then assessed and approved to have the boys' baby sister, Mia. Introductions with her were over a seven-day period and were very different as we were already parents. I remember meeting her and turning to Daniel and saying that she reminded me of Tom. I think that this helped to feel a connection with her from the start. I was so excited for the boys to meet her, as were they, and they were keen to "help" do things for her. They also enjoyed playing with her toys. What really helped was that we were allowed to have a significant part in the planning for introductions with Mia as it needed to fit around the boys as Jack was in school and George and Tom were in nursery.*

Moving Mia was the hardest of our four as she had no concept of why she was moving and who we were. She attached to me quickly and would cry if I moved away from her. Tom found this particularly difficult as he had been the youngest of his siblings and loved to snuggle up with me, but suddenly he was competing with a baby. Their relationship has taken time to develop and it has only been since they have been in school together that it has become stronger.

PLANNING MOVES

Sometimes children who currently live together are to be placed separately in new permanent families. In other situations, children who are currently in separate placements are to be reunited or united into a permanent new family. In each case, careful thought needs to be given to how to prepare children and families, and how to manage introductions and placement. The logistics of preparing a new family for the placement of a large sibling group such as a group of three or more children, and managing introductions, may be especially challenging for adopters. Some agencies and writers have advocated that it may be better not to place a large group of siblings simultaneously but there is no available research to support this either way. It is, however, important to share practice experience and to consider the issues carefully for each child and for the adoptive family.

The knowledge that you have obtained in completing the sibling assessment should help inform the introductions plan. It will be helpful to think about each child's needs and any tendency for one or more children to vie for adult attention. For example, Argent (2008) suggested that it was important to consider how the group deals with stress and conflict and how each child reacts to pressure, and proposed that social workers address questions such as:

- Do siblings recognise each other's distress and comfort each other?
- Do they close ranks against outsiders?
- Do they forgive each other for real or imagined transgressions?
- Does any one child take responsibility, or blame, for the actions of all?
- Can each child express feelings, wishes and opinions or is there a spokesperson?
- Is play boisterous and pleasurable or competitive and aggressive?
- Which children "gang up", "pair off", or appear to be "loners"?
- How and to whom do individual children show affection?
- Does one child "wind the others up" or get them into trouble?

- Who shares and who does not?
- Who copies whom and how do siblings describe each other?
- How does each child rank in the sibling group and gain adults' attention?

(Adapted from *Ten Top Tips on Placing Siblings*, Argent, 2008)

The answers to these questions and others will have an impact on how the introductions should be planned and managed for a group of brothers and sisters as they get ready to meet their prospective new family.

In *Ten Top Tips for Making Introductions*, Dunbar (2009, p32) suggested the following good practice points specifically with regard to siblings:

- *Take time to get to know each child and the dynamics of the sibling group before any decisions about introductions are made.*

- *Work with each child separately and also as part of a group when preparing them for introductions.*

- *Be flexible during introductions and placement, particularly if a large sibling group is being placed; consider "serial" placements or placing children in pairs rather than as one group.*

- *Consider each child's needs separately and as a group: should each child spend time alone with their new carers/parents during introductions? Should separated brothers and sisters be reunited before introductions begin?*

- *Remember, every introduction of a sibling group will be different, and the more children involved, the more complex the questions and decisions will be.*

Brothers and sisters in the same foster home

It is vital that enough time is built into the process for new parents to learn about each child as an individual, prior to meeting them, as well as how they get on with each other. The family needs the opportunity to read about, talk about and think about each child as they would if they were considering a single child. Each child will have his or her own history and own unique experience of family life. He or she will have their own particular needs and time must be taken, for instance, to meet therapists, doctors, teachers or others who can contribute information on the individual child. The child's current carers will have invaluable information and it may well be that several meetings rather than the usual one are needed before the adopters meet the children, to talk with the foster carers about each individual child as well as how they function as a group in the context of this particular foster family.

The benefits of pre-meets (meetings between prospective adopters and children prior to matching; also known as one-off meetings, chemistry meets, bump-into days or mini-meets) should be considered as these may help to make first meetings less intense. Pre-meets can give adopters an opportunity to observe the siblings rather than having to focus on engagement and interaction.

The new parents should probably meet *all* the children together on the first occasion. However, opportunities should be built into the introductory process to allow time with each child individually as well. Introductions are always tiring and quite stressful but are likely to be even more so when a number of children are involved at the same time. It is vital that support is available from the agency in practical ways, e.g. help with transport, and also that time is made available for discussion and reflection.

One or more children may vie for individual attention, whilst another may hide behind a sofa or leave the room. Thinking about how to include each child's needs and balancing this with time for the children to be together with their new family will be central considerations when planning introductions.

Some key points to consider:

- There should be an opportunity to look at the adopters' "family book" and any filmed material that they prepared for the children, as well as looking at the children's life story materials together.

- If children compete with each other, consider the merit of each child having a small special task or responsibility to help structure initial time with the adopters, as well as some joint activities. This can be planned ahead so that foster carers have some idea about what will be happening as well as spontaneous activities and play. For example, one child might be asked to show the adopters around the garden and the outdoor play equipment, whilst another could then be asked to show their prospective adopters where their bedroom is. Both children can show their adopters some photos of their last holiday with the foster family.

- Consider how and when each child should spend some time alone with their future parent/s during introductions.

- Visits to nursery and school can include prospective adopters seeing examples of each child's work, art, crafts, reading and writing levels.

Plans to reunite brothers and sisters who are currently not living together

The work that will need to be undertaken will depend on the extent to which the children are familiar with one another, for example, are they used to spending extended periods of time together on a weekly basis? Are they used to having overnight stays or not?

Key issues to address:

- Is it possible and/or advisable to reunite the children in one of their foster homes prior to adoption introductions commencing? This will be a complex decision as there are bound to be some losses as well as potential gains associated with any move. The time that you have between making the permanence plan and likely placement with adopters will need to be taken into account as will the relationships between the carers and what each can offer.

- Contact plans should be reviewed. It will probably be important for the children to spend more time together and for this to increase incrementally in the lead up to permanent placement. The use of pictorial calendars with child-friendly stickers (teddies, etc) can help young children to "see" when contact or overnight stays are planned.

- If the children have not already had some contact that involved staying overnight, then it will be crucial to address this now. Ideally, children should have shared experiences of meal times, deciding what activities to do together or not, getting ready for bed, getting up in the morning, and so on. More time spent together is likely to make it easier for them and the adoptive parent/s when introductions begin.

MOVING IN ALL TOGETHER OR NOT?

There may be differing views between fostering, adoption and child care staff about the merits of how and when to place a group of brothers and sisters. For example: should children be placed at the same time all together? Are there any advantages in placing an older child first, as some have suggested that this might help to give younger children permission to move, and/or to settle into adoptive family life more easily? Research does not provide any clear-cut answers. In general terms, if children are in the same foster home, it is unlikely to be in their interests not to place them all together and they would find it hard to understand a staged move for one or more of them. For children who are currently living apart and the plan is to reunite them, the views of staff who know the children well, and the views of foster carers and adoptive parents and their ideas, should always be considered. Everyone is much more likely to fully engage and support a plan in which they have had an active part. There is no single answer that will be right for all separated siblings.

Whether or not the children are all placed with their adoptive family at the same time, it will always be crucial to involve children so that they

share a sense of commitment and common purpose. Children need to know what is happening and this should be openly discussed with them, their foster carers and adopters. Argent (2008, p25) provided an example of this happening:

> One local authority had found a family to take five siblings aged between four and 11. All the children were introduced to the new family, shown where they would live and even where they would sleep. They were included in the planning sessions and agreed that the oldest should move in first 'so that she would be able to help the others to settle because she would know her way around'. The remaining siblings made frequent visits to their new home, and helped to get their rooms ready until the middle two moved in together. The two youngest joined them six weeks later after several overnight stays. They all felt part of their special placement project.

Whilst being open to considering a range of placement options, the possibility of resentment and misunderstanding needs to be carefully addressed. Dunbar (2009, p30) recognised the need for flexibility:

> Perhaps very large sibling groups could join their new family in pairs – this gives more time and space for preparation and for initial relationships to be made. But this approach has to be balanced against the resentment and heightened sibling rivalry established children and newcomers might feel towards each other.

Think about how to include each child's needs and balancing this with time for the children to be together with their new family will be central considerations when planning introductions.

There is no easy tried and tested formula that will meet the needs of all sibling groups; rather, there are key ingredients that need to be considered before plans are made.

CHILDREN IN SEPARATE PLACEMENTS AND WHERE CONTINUED PLACEMENT APART IS PLANNED

When brothers and sisters have already been living apart, much of the work that is needed now will depend on the children's current understanding of why they are living apart. Perhaps older children may appear to have coped with separation but understood that this was only temporary. Children may have been reassured by the knowledge that they would see younger siblings every week. Learning that siblings will be placed permanently apart from them may understandably provoke very different feelings. All children will sometimes have shown anger and upset a sibling at some point. It is important that latent feelings and misunderstandings that children may harbour are anticipated and addressed. The explanations that are given now may have a long reach for children in the years ahead.

Key issues to address

- The timing of direct work with each child to explain plans.

- Any changes to contact after the permanency plan is made.

- Information and photos of the children's adoptive and permanent carers to be shown/shared with all children unless safeguarding prevents this from happening.

- How and when the adopters of one or more children will meet the child's other siblings and their carers.

- Plans that clearly set out how the children's relationship will continue. The use of pictorial calendars with stickers can help young children to "see" when contact will be happening even if there may be long gaps. Skype, video calls and exchange of video clips or DVDs should be considered especially if face-to-face contact is inadvisable.

- Life story work should include explanations and family photos with key information about all siblings. A clear and consistent account of decisions should be provided to all those involved.

CHILDREN CURRENTLY PLACED TOGETHER WHO ARE TO GO TO SEPARATE PERMANENT FAMILIES

Clearly, any decision to place separately children who are currently together should be based on a careful and thorough assessment of their needs and relationship, and should involve the children as well as the current carers.

Children and carers will also need to be involved in discussion about what happens next and about the family-finding process. It could be, for example, that a younger child is going to be placed for adoption as soon as possible while an older child is to have a period of work or therapy prior to moving on. The children will need to be prepared for what is to happen and their needs considered at each stage, for example, how will an older child be involved when their younger sibling/s meet their prospective new family? The way in which adopters are prepared, not only for the child/ren to be placed with them but also to be able to hold the needs of other siblings in mind, can make a big difference.

Adopters should be given the opportunity to think about how they can engage with siblings who will not be joining their family but will always be important and with whom they will hopefully be supporting contact. Practices that can help include:

- an introductory letter from the adopters, including some photos of them;
- adopters meeting older/other siblings and photos of this happening early on;
- older/other siblings having information about the adopters and the opportunity to ask their social worker questions (How will I know that they will be nice? How can I know that they won't hurt my little sister?)

KEY PRACTICE POINTS

- Think about what preparation each child will need and the timing of this. If parents, birth relatives or an older sibling "know" of the plan before younger children do, what is the risk that information will be passed on? Relatives who are angry and upset about the decision may blurt out information during contact.

- Consider what meaning the placement decision will have for each child: think about whether there is a risk that one or more of the children might blame another for this happening.

- Consider how each child can be helped to achieve an understanding of the ways in which their relationship will continue after they are living apart.

- Set out plans that show how the children's relationships will continue. The use of pictorial calendars with stickers can help young children to "see" when contact will be happening even if there may be long gaps sometimes.

- Life story work should include explanations and family photos with significant information about all siblings. A clear and consistent account of decisions should be provided to all those affected.

Chapter 9
Brothers and sisters: visits and keeping in touch

After decisions have been made as to permanent placement, contact plans should be reviewed. For example, when children have been separated in foster care but are to be placed together for adoption or alternative placements, it is likely to be helpful to increase the frequency and duration of visits, including spending overnights together. When children are already placed apart and continued placement apart is planned, there may need to be a corresponding reduction or change in contact. Whatever the immediate issues in terms of planning adoption or other placements, the needs, risks and benefits associated with contact – and therefore, sustaining, or not, relationships – in the longer term will also need to be carefully assessed and planned.

If children have to be placed apart from one or more siblings, it will be crucial that everyone understands why this has happened and that planning continues to support each child and their sibling relationships.

After decisions have been made about how the siblings are to be placed, the well-being of children and how they adjust will be influenced by the quality of work that continues to be undertaken with them and on their behalf. Key components at this stage are that:

- explanations are provided for children through direct work, life story/life history materials and later life letters. Explanations, knowledge and understanding are important for all looked after children – and the decision to separate will need particularly sensitive work;

- all of the children's carers/adopters should have a detailed understanding of the reasons why separate placements were planned so that they are able to talk about this;

- consideration should be given to matched placements wherever possible when children are to be placed separately for adoption, that is, adopters who ideally share some similar values and attitudes as well as a commitment to the children's continuing relationship;

- families should meet one another as soon as possible, they should know how to contact one another and be involved at each stage so that they can fully support what is being planned;

- contact plans should be robust, carefully considered, negotiated and supported. Visits to include overnight stays at a family-friendly venue, such as at a caravan site, should be discussed positively unless there are clear safeguarding or other reasons to prevent this;

- interventions should address any difficulties that contributed to separation, for example, high levels of conflict between brothers and sisters, as this will also be likely to impact on children's capacity to make and sustain friendships;

- children should have information and tangible reassurance about their siblings: photos; videos; have opportunities to meet their carers/ adoptive family; know how their siblings are; and know how they will maintain relationships through visits and other links.

When considering how children's sibling relationships can best be supported following separation, it will be important to think flexibly. For example, Neil *et al* (2020) recently recommended that the use of digital methods, including video calling and a digitally mediated post-adoption letterbox contact service, should be considered as part of a range of options available for children separated from their birth families.

The meaning of contact and its importance to each child within a sibling group may vary at any point in time and over time. Meeting up with brothers and sisters can help children talk about past trauma that they endured, which can be helpful but also carries the potential for negative emotions to resurface for, and between, some children. As children become increasingly settled and secure in separate adoptive families, their views about how often they want to see siblings may change with some wanting less contact. Some children want to "move on from their past, but even so, it is usually important to maintain links for the future and to recognise that needs and the significance of contact may ebb and flow at different developmental stages.

PLANNING AND SUPPORTING CONTACT

In order to work well and to endure, contact requires careful planning and support. Over the years ahead, the reliability and predictability of contact will be crucially important as these factors are associated with adopted people's "satisfaction" with contact, and more so than its type (Neil *et al*, 2013). Conversely, gaps in contact, contact ending, or not knowing what is happening about visits is likely to be difficult for children and young people. The level and type of contact that can be achieved will clearly need to take account of a range of considerations based on an assessment of benefits and possible risks.

Macaskill (2002) and others have also noted the importance of effective planning and support so that potential difficulties can be minimised or managed effectively. Beckett (2002) set out key issues in assessing and planning sibling contact that have been adapted and summarised here:

- The child's individual needs as well as relationships within the sibling group must be assessed, for example, the roles children may have had within their family of origin. A care-giving child who remains in foster care may be used to taking care of and "organising" their younger siblings. Adopters of the younger children will need to be prepared and helped to think through how best to manage this.

- What can we learn and reasonably anticipate from the children's background histories, their previous and current behaviour? For example, if there has been a history of sexual abuse in the family, what impact has this had on how a child perceives and relates to siblings?

- What is the purpose of contact? Everyone should be clear about the reasons why contact is being planned. For example, it is important to consider not only the children's current relationship but also to recognise potential benefits in respect of contact and maintaining links over the long term. Some brothers and sisters may not appear very close now but maintaining links allows the relationship to develop in the future. Identity, talking about shared family history and related aspects may become more important as children mature and "recycle" aspects of their earlier experiences in their family of origin.

- Are there any specific risks and how can these be managed and minimised? For example, safe care practices should be integral when planning contact between siblings if sexual abuse is known to have taken place or there are concerns that it may have occurred.

- Do some, but not all, of the children have contact with adult birth relatives? If so, what are the potential implications of this? Risks must be understood in context rather than blanket assumptions made. For example, an older sibling who retains contact with family may also have acted protectively and disclosed abuse to protect younger siblings.

Drawing on studies of contact after adoption, Neil *et al* (2015) set out a practice model for planning and supporting contact (see www.uea.ac.uk/contact-after-adoption/resources). In their model, they provide a helpful guide to practitioners. The principles underpinning the model are:

1. that contact should be **_purposeful_** (how contact can benefit the child is the central question);

2. that contact should be **_individualised_** (taking account of the child's particular needs, and of particular characteristics of the children, adoptive parents and birth relatives as these can have a bearing on contact), and

3. that contact is a ***relationship-based*** process that is ***dynamic*** across time.

   All relevant parties should be involved in some way: the adoptive parents, the adopted child, where old enough, and the birth relatives. Even quite young children can be involved in some way. They might choose between a manageable "shortlist" of options provided by their parents as to where they meet; what sort of games and toys they take to play with/show siblings; what photos they share of themselves and some special times or events such as holidays or a birthday since they last met up; a drawing or painting they might select to give to a brother or sister; a birthday card or postcard they might want to send, etc.

   The Contact after Adoption website (https://contact.rip.org.uk) draws on extensive research by Neil *et al* at the University of East Anglia that looked at adopted children's contact with birth relatives after adoption and what arrangements are like from the point of view of children, adopters and birth relatives. The website was developed in collaboration with Research in Practice and practitioners across England, to share expertise and produce accessible and practical resources for workers. The website covers the following topics:

   - planning contact for children;
   - listening to and including children's wishes during planning;
   - supporting birth relatives in understanding and maintaining contact;
   - supporting adopters to understand the importance and benefits of contact and manage plans.

   For each topic, there is a mixture of research briefings, practice guides, presentations, exercises and tools for working with families. A number of case studies and films of interviews with families are included. The Practice Brief, *Listening to Very Young Children when Planning and Reviewing Contact,* provides a focus when considering contact from each child's perspective. A section on planning and maintaining contact between siblings in different placements is being developed.

PLANNING CONTACT – POINTERS FROM RESEARCH

Contact will always require individual assessment. Research is based on populations of children and can provide some helpful guidance but it is crucially important to understand different risks and possible benefits based on each child's experiences, wants and needs.

There is evidence to suggest that when children are permanently placed at a young age, for example, for adoption, their short- and particularly long-term needs for birth family connections can be overlooked because they are too young to express a view about contact. In this context, Ryan (2020, p.4) highlighted the following key points to note from research:

- Even when contact is challenging and painful, it may be wanted and valued – this needs to be distinguished from contact that is harmful to children.

- The needs and views of children will change over time.

- Where children are too young to express their wishes and feelings, it is especially important to consider their potential long-term contact needs.

- Some children may express their feelings about family contact through their behaviour, for example, appearing happy and relaxed in contact – or conversely fearful and disturbed.

- Relationships are dynamic.

- Family and friendship networks are complex for all of us, but particularly for children separated from their families, and contact with relatives in the wider network can be greatly valued by children.

The importance of skilled professional support was emphasised as central to helping both manage challenges and facilitating good quality visits and links between children.

Macaskill (2002) highlighted that children need to understand professional decisions about splitting them from siblings – if this work is not done, unresolved issues are likely to adversely affect sibling contact. She also identified that:

- Sibling contact is different to contact with adult birth relatives because it does not produce the same emotional aftermath and consequently has the potential to be sustained at a higher level than four times annually; however, it is vital that the frequency is practically manageable for all the parties involved.

- Sibling contact is more likely to be sustainable between children placed in different adoptive families when adopters are compatible in terms of class, values and aspirations. Wide differences and tensions between the adopters are liable to drive a wedge between brothers and sisters.

- Sibling contact is a predominantly positive experience for the majority of children and works better when there is more emotional warmth and good interaction between them.

- Children generally want more contact with siblings, even when these relationships are sometimes far from straightforward.

- The ending of a significant sibling relationship is deeply traumatic for some children:

The most deeply traumatised children in this study were those who had undertaken a protective role for a sibling while living in the birth family and who found that sibling relationship severed against their wishes.

(Macaskill, 2002, p96)

Other studies report clearer benefits associated with continuing contact between brothers and sisters than have been identified in respect of birth parent contact after adoption. In a very helpful systematic review of 11 UK studies, Boyle (2017) examined the impact of birth family contact on adopted children. In nearly all cases where contact between children and birth parents was problematic, contact with siblings and grandparents was positive (2017, p28):

Sibling contact was consistently identified by adoptive parents, foster carers and children as very important. It was also thought that this attachment was a significant protective factor in the absence of secure attachments to birth parents. The wish to see more of siblings and concern for separated siblings was a salient theme for children across the board.

Iyer *et al* (2020, p39) reviewed research and found that insufficient priority was given to facilitating contact between looked after or adopted children and young people. They emphasised that the key question was not whether or how much contact, but rather how best to facilitate positive experiences and meaningful involvement:

Family-centred approaches to contact, including contact which is more "family-like" rather than formal, can also involve recognising and supporting important relationships within a broad and dynamic conceptualisation of family. There are of course risks and benefits to be weighed in all kinds of contact, but in particular, the reviewed evidence demonstrates that well-facilitated contact with siblings is associated with better sibling relationships, a positive effect on children's mental health and can support ongoing relationships with birth families, through childhood and into adulthood.

In respect of children placed apart from some of their siblings, contact may have been planned but had not yet taken place. As Meakings *et al* (2018) noted in this regard and more generally:

Whilst adoptive parents were often determined to help strengthen sibling bonds created and affected by adoption, this commitment was not always championed through social work intervention.

KEY POINTS

- The most common form of face-to-face after adoption contact is that between birth siblings (Selwyn, 2004).

- About half of children placed for adoption lost contact with their brothers and sisters either on placement or soon afterwards (Jones and Henderson, 2017; Neil *et al*, 2018).

- Sibling contact arrangements and children's wishes are poorly documented (Jones and Henderson, 2017).

- There is little consideration of indirect ways of maintaining links such as through phone calls, postcards or similar means (Rushton *et al*, 2001).

- Adopters broadly support contact between brothers and sisters in different placements unless it poses a clear threat (Barth and Berry, 1988; Rushton *et al*, 2001).

- Studies report much clearer benefits associated with continuing contact between brothers and sisters than have been identified in respect of birth parent contact after adoption (Boyle, 2017).

- Adoptive parents are usually not satisfied if sibling contact is not occurring (Neil *et al*, 2018).

- Face-to-face contact with siblings is positive for the majority of families where it occurs (Neil *et al*, 2018). However, families are not getting the support that they need (Meakings *et al*, 2018).

CONTACT BETWEEN ADOPTED CHILDREN AND SIBLINGS IN LONG-TERM FOSTER CARE/WITH FAMILY MEMBERS

Planning for "no contact" may sometimes seem to be the safest option. Social workers may focus on the possible risks of continuing sibling contact when older siblings remain in foster care and younger ones are placed for adoption. Typically, the older siblings will retain some level of contact with parents. However, continuing contact with parents should *not* be used as a blanket reason to terminate sibling contact. Ending contact between brothers and sisters involves risks and losses for children and their families, for example, young children may be distressed, resent contact ending and find it very hard to settle or trust their adoptive parents. There is a danger that risks and losses are insufficiently recognised and considered. Contact issues should always be fully explored, allowing for flexibility and openness. Potential risks and gains, benefits and losses should be assessed and carefully balanced. Some risks may be small and manageable. Safeguards and commitment to contact can reduce risks.

IS THERE TOO MUCH FOCUS ON RISK AND NOT ENOUGH ON BENEFITS?

Dibben *et al* (2018, p14) found that:

The focus on contact for siblings separated by adoption was a strong and enduring theme across the professional groups, and there was a clear sense that there must be better ways of ensuring that this can be managed in adoption for the benefit of sibling groups.

Despite this and the potential benefits of contact, Neil *et al* (2018, p174) highlighted variations in contact that was planned and raised questions about more recent practice in this regard, noting that:

In terms of differences in contact planning, there were indications in the data that more contact was taking place for children who were aged two or over at placement, for those who had been adopted more than five years ago, and those who were adopted from certain local authorities.

There may be particular wariness or pessimism in respect of planning and managing contact when siblings are in different types of placement and when contact with birth parents may continue for some whilst ending for others. Thoburn (2018, p31) set out six commonly-held but "unevidenced myths" identified by researchers who have interviewed practitioners. One of these was:

Contact between children in long-term placements and siblings living with or in contact with adult birth relatives is likely to be harmful to a child in an adoptive or planned "part of the family" foster family placement.

Adopters' attitudes, levels of comfort and capacity to exercise some control over arrangements are likely to be factors that interact and overlap. Research by Neil *et al* (2018) has summarised that the most helpful approach by agencies seemed to be one that supported and empowered participants to find an arrangement that worked for them, rather than dictating a standard approach.

Contact with siblings assisted the adopted children to be reassured about their birth siblings' welfare, promoted identity and belonging, and in some cases provided a positive model of parenting for older siblings. However, it also raised issues for the adopted children about why they were separated from their brothers and sisters and the reasons for their levels of contact with them. Adoptive parents were concerned about risk to their child in a small minority of cases where a sibling had previously abused them.

However, without the knowledge of siblings and/or an opportunity to build the foundation of a meaningful relationship in childhood, significant barriers are often present in adulthood to developing positive and meaningful relationships with birth brothers and sisters.

(Taken from Stage 1 of the Contact After Adoption research: see www.uea.ac.uk/contact-after-adoption)

Empathy and adopter communicative openness are crucially important. These qualities are positively linked not only with sustaining birth family contact but also with adopted people having a cohesive sense of identity.

The ways in which contact between siblings is considered during preparation stages and subsequently will have an impact on shaping some applicants' attitudes, whilst others – perhaps most – may begin the process feeling positive about contact between siblings. Social workers may sometimes focus on possible risks and events that might occur, without maintaining a sufficient balance on losses that would be sustained if contact ends. Adopters provided suggestions for improving contact (Neil *et al*, 2018, p172), which included the following:

- Provide greater support to encourage sibling contact. Do not assume adopters/carers will be proactive, e.g. 'We are too stressed and busy day to day to get on top of it. It would be better for us if his Independent Reviewing Officer just directed the social worker to plan two dates a year, venue, etc, and then we could just come along to it.'

- More encouragement to promote face-to-face contact (especially with siblings) despite the anxieties it may provoke in adopters.

- More sharing between workers involved with different siblings.

SPECIALIST ORGANISATIONS HELPING SIBLINGS TO MEET UP

A range of organisations provide specialist services for siblings, for example, After Adoption and Open Nest, whilst other organisations have been specifically established to help promote sibling contact.

The Siblings Together Buddy project was set up in 2013 to reunite siblings separated through care and adoption. The scheme uses trained volunteers as Buddies able to support and encourage siblings to enjoy activities together on a monthly basis. Aims of the scheme include helping to improve communication and relationships between children as well as for them to have fun together. The project was evaluated by Sebba (2017). Key findings included that: young people enjoyed the sibling contact and wanted more frequent contact and for longer; most sibling relationships improved; and children and young people developed greater confidence and were able to offer support to one another. Siblings developed their sense of identity as part of a family through sharing jointly experienced histories, and also benefitted from being able to talk about future plans and relationships with siblings and Buddies.

Recommendations for policy and practice included:

- give siblings, placed separately in care, informal opportunities to meet and participate in activities;

- provide support for siblings to meet in order to ensure safeguarding but not to impose formal contact;

- use volunteers who are trained and supported to undertake this role;

- fund activities and travel to enable them to meet – this is an investment in developing greater placement stability and increasing well-being.

Stand Up For Siblings is a Scotland-wide collaboration between child welfare, children's rights and legal organisations and academics. It aims to value, protect and promote the well-being of brothers and sisters who become looked after or who are at risk of this happening. The organisation aims to influence the law, policy and practice.

KEY PRACTICE POINTS

- Be clear about the importance of relationships between brothers and sisters in early discussions with potential new families. The way in which prospective adopters receive information about contact plans and the content of the information can have a significant impact on their views.

- Be clear about the purpose of contact and communicate this well – remember that even if children squabble and fall out now, their relationship can develop in the years ahead.

- Be positive about contact between brothers and sisters: adopters broadly support contact between brothers and sisters in different placements unless it poses a clear threat.

- Involve adopters in planning contact and ensure that they meet the adopters of their children's sibling/s early on. Bear in mind that adopters who share similar values, attitudes and aspirations are more likely to work well together to manage contact for children in separate families.

- Address practical problems such as venues, timing and costs – ensuring that contact occurs requires positive social work planning and support.

- Consider indirect means of maintaining links between visits such as through phone or video calls, Skype, social media platforms, sending postcards and similar means.
- Remember that the impact and risks of not having contact also need to be part of any assessment.

Chapter 10
Research: how children and their families fare

INTRODUCTION

This chapter draws on research to identify key needs and explores issues faced by children and their families. A brief generic overview is followed by a focus on some issues that are particularly relevant to sibling placements. The importance of planning the right sort of support at the right time in order to help promote the best outcomes for children and families is addressed in Chapter 11.

OVERVIEW – CHILDREN'S FAMILY BACKGROUNDS, THEIR PRE-PLACEMENT EXPERIENCES AND NEEDS

Neil *et al* (2018, p114) summarised factors associated with poorer outcomes for children needing permanent placements overall, as follows:

- higher levels of maltreatment;
- children showing moderate or high levels of distress when moved from the foster carer to the adoptive family;
- children spending more than 12 months in care;
- children having two or more foster homes before moving to their adoptive family;
- children who had been exposed to drugs or alcohol *in utero*;
- children whose birth parents had a learning disability.

Neil *et al* noted that their findings reflected much of the earlier research on adoption, that is: age at placement affects outcomes for children though the extent and timing of early adversity may be more important than age at placement on its own.

127

Older children were more likely to have higher SDQ scores. Children with particularly high levels of emotional and behavioural needs are reported as not doing very well. These children had a score of 20 or more on the SDQ total difficulties score (the general population average is 8).

As set out earlier in this guide, SDQ findings can help inform the assessment process as well as help to identify what behavioural intervention and support might be needed. Some of the research cited in this section highlights the significance of SDQ scores and their links with outcomes.

Recent research has also focused on Adverse Childhood Experiences (ACEs), which are strongly related to various risk factors including health in adult life. Most children who are placed for adoption have been exposed to multiple ACEs. The Wales Adoption Study (Meakings *et al*, 2017b, 2018) found that just over half of children in the study had experienced four or more ACEs, with neglect being the most common. They identified a relationship between the number of ACEs children experienced and emotional problems at one year after placement. There were associations between the number of days children spent with their birth parents and children's hyperactivity and emotional behaviour problems afterwards. Similarly, the more days children spent in care, the more emotional behaviour problems were evident at follow up.

Saunders *et al* (2013) highlighted some important practice points to consider in respect of sibling placements: the need for a clear understanding of the demands as well as the rewards that each child might bring; an understanding of the "cumulative impact" presented by the sibling group; the importance of emotional warmth shown by adopters in the face of behavioural challenges; and the need to develop ways of helping children make and sustain friendships.

INTRODUCTIONS AND THE EARLY DAYS

Getting off to a good start matters. Foster carers are crucially important in facilitating a good start for both adopters and children and this aspect was set out in Chapter 8. Research on outcomes has considered the experiences of adoptive families. In their study, Selwyn *et al* (2014, p11) highlighted what many families tell us: introductions are tiring and the adjustments required in the first few months and beyond can feel overwhelming:

> *Adopters often describe the first few weeks of an adoptive placement as exhausting and like a whirlwind and parents in this study were no exception. It is therefore important that adoptive parents are bolstered pre-placement, feel well supported, and are strengthened for what is to come.*

The research also identified that sadly it was not unusual for adopters to have some concerns about the quality of foster care that their child/ren had experienced: two-fifths of parents had misgivings about this whilst more than two-thirds felt that important information had not been shared or had not been fully explained to them. More recently, the Wales Adoption Study (Meakings et al, 2017, 2018) found similarly – see Chapter 8 for more detail and practice suggestions.

THE "CARE-GIVER" CHILD

Children may have developed care-giving behaviours that served them well in their birth family but are no longer "needed" and may be viewed very differently within their adoptive family. In the past, older, caring brothers and sisters may have had their own fragile sense of self-esteem and worth bolstered by feeling needed and wanted by younger siblings. Even when these behaviours had diminished during placement in foster care, it is important to bear in mind that moves can trigger insecurities. Previous patterns of behaviour may re-emerge. Older brothers and sisters may feel that they need to "take charge" once again.

Rushton et al (2001) referred to the issue of "parentification" in their study of families with siblings in permanent placement. They found that this behaviour was a common source of concern to parents in the early months but was relatively short-lived in most cases. However, in respect of contact, Macaskill (2002) identified that this behaviour was more persistent and difficult in some contact relationships between brothers and sisters; she suggested that it may be easier for parents and carers to address the issue when children were all placed together.

The Wales Adoption Study (Meakings et al, 2017a) noted that:

> It should not be surprising that siblings with difficult shared early experiences may exhibit controlling and parentified behaviours. In an attempt to stay safe and feel more in command of their own care and protection, some maltreated children seek to prevent carers from being in control by themselves displaying controlling behaviour (Howe, 2009). There is an irony that some of the sibling challenges reported by parents in adoptive family life were the very dynamics that may have helped to reassure and possibly protect children whilst living in the birth family or foster care placements.

It is important to recognise that families wanted help in managing and promoting sibling relationships but this was often lacking.

CHILDREN'S SIBLING AND PEER RELATIONSHIPS

Research over many years tells us that emotionally fraught relationships between children are especially challenging for adopters to manage. Rushton *et al* (2001) found that those children who had difficulties in their interactions with their siblings were not necessarily scoring highly in respect of child–parent interaction problems. Selwyn *et al* (2014, p13) identified that children with marked difficulties in their sibling relationships figured more prominently in adoption breakdowns, that is, the "left home" group:

> *Sibling relationships were considered typical for the majority of children, but just under half (48%) of the children who had left home and 18% of the "at home" group were in constant conflict with brothers or sisters. Warring siblings created splits in some families with one parent caring for the study child and the other parenting the remaining siblings.*

The study found that the presence of siblings was not associated with disruption. However, in a subsequent reanalysis of the interview data, Selwyn (2018) reviewed whether sibling relationships had influenced the outcomes. It is important to bear in mind that this work focused on a sample of adoptive placements in England and Wales that had broken down post-adoption order or that were in crisis. Siblings were defined as the children with whom the "index child" had grown up – whether by birth or through adoption. Hence, this included some children placed at the same time as one or more siblings, a sibling placed for adoption at a later date, and sibling relationships that were created between the placed child and the adopter's own birth child/ren. Whilst conflictual sibling relationships were not seen by adopters as the main cause of disruption, the majority of placements that were in crisis or had broken down were indirectly influenced by abusive sibling relationships. Parents described these relationships as "toxic" or "dysfunctional". Aggression had not diminished as children grew up. The importance of recognising and addressing aggression early on was emphasised.

In another study that included single children and sibling groups, Neil *et al* (2018) found that, whilst most school-aged children got on at least reasonably well with peers, children in secondary school had more problems. When children had difficulties in school, problems with peers were often part of the overall picture. Neil *et al* (2018, p62) cited a quote that summed up some common themes expressed by parents. These centred on their children's emotional difficulties in developing and navigating relationships with others:

> *Child struggles to understand how relationships work – struggles with empathy and understanding the feelings of others. Presents as difficult and disruptive when worried or frightened. Attempts to be in control to make themselves feel safe. Very competitive for attention or resources.*

> *Challenges decisions and struggles to trust adults...Struggles with sense of identity so tends to copy others.*

It is also important to remember the impact on children who were often both aware of and distressed by their difficulties:

> *He struggles to maintain friendships with children his own age. Feels very emotionally upset when friendships break down. Desperate to be liked by friends and adults (particularly in school).*

AGGRESSION, EMOTIONAL REGULATION AND SIBLING CONFLICTS

Selwyn *et al* (2014, p28) cited studies that had examined the factors that increase the risk of child aggression, such as exposure to domestic violence, paternal behaviours, neglect under the age of two, and exposure to alcohol *in utero*, and noted that it was important to:

> *Identify young children who are aggressive in foster care and intervene to address the aggression. The message from research on aggression in general population samples is that most children will not "grow out of it".*

Meakings *et al* (2017b, p1781) noted that siblings typically shared a history of maltreatment and many 'had complex, often conflictual relationships', but the presence of birth siblings in the adoptive home also provided support and comfort for children. New sibling relationships, created by placing children into families with existing children, also resulted in a mix of advantages and complications.

The study echoed other research (Rushton, 2001; Saunders and Selwyn, 2010; Selwyn *et al*, 2014; Neil *et al*, 2018) in reporting that physical aggression shown between the children was of particular concern to parents. However, the aggression was sometimes explained by parents in the context of describing children who struggled with close relationships and were emotionally dysregulated, with poor impulse control, and quick to vent frustration – including using physical aggression – towards parents, peers, pets and others. Adoptive parents described a common theme whereby children seemed to need to control, or try to control – this behaviour was particularly evident during sibling play. Children found it hard to compromise or had difficulty co-operating with others, as one parent described (Meakings *et al*, 2017b, p1781):

> *Stacey is the boss and she expects to be able to be in control all the time... She needs to be in control, but they're both controlling, very controlling. And I think probably in the past, she's kept that control and Freddie [younger brother] has gone along with it, but now he's actually saying 'No'.*

Even though adopters viewed children's sibling relationships as more conflictual than agreeable, they still valued the bond that their children had and wanted to strengthen this in the years ahead. However, parents felt that they were not getting the help they wanted to achieve this.

SUMMARY OF KEY RESEARCH FINDINGS

- Most adopters felt positively about the decision to keep siblings together and would recommend sibling adoption (Saunders *et al*, 2013).

- Most adopters felt warmly towards their children despite the behavioural difficulties that they presented. Lower warmth tended to be expressed for older siblings with very challenging behaviour (Saunders *et al*, 2013; Neil *et al*, 2018).

- Physical aggression shown between the children was of particular concern to parents (Rushton *et al*, 2001; Selwyn *et al*, 2014; Meakings *et al*, 2018; Neil *et al*, 2018).

- Most adopters described sibling relationships as being fairly typical with highs and lows but "constant conflict" between siblings was associated with higher rates of adoption breakdown (Selwyn *et al*, 2014). This conflict had usually been apparent from early in the placement. Parents described the most troubling behaviours as: physical aggression largely instigated by one child; coercion; and sexualised behaviour between siblings.

- Adoptions were more stable when parents reported that the children were equally responsible for causing conflict, which was more typically verbal rather than physical.

- The number of siblings with difficulties (rather than the severity of an individual child's difficulties) was associated with the placement being rated as having major difficulties (Saunders *et al*, 2013).

- Sibling adopters caring for children with higher SDQ scores were more likely to experience anxiety and depression as they struggled to cope with trying to meet *all* their children's needs (Saunders *et al*, 2013).

- While many children had difficulties, adopters were also able to identify prosocial behaviours, such as sharing readily and being kind to younger children (Saunders *et al*, 2013; Neil *et al*, 2018).

- Problems in peer relationships was a significant difficulty for some children (Saunders *et al*, 2013). Neil *et al* (2018) described how parents viewed this in terms of their children being of lower developmental age than their peers and having difficulty understanding how relationships work. Their child/ren's poor social skills also tended to mean that sometimes other children avoided them.

Chapter 11
Planning the right support for children and families

INTRODUCTION

Many groups of brothers and sisters will blossom and do well within their adoptive family and their parents will experience far more rewards than difficulties. Some families will need little formal support, but for others the availability of a range of family and agency support can make the difference between children and adopters thriving or barely managing to keep going. We know that the reasons for adoptions breaking down are complex. We also know that most families show huge warmth and commitment, and keep going even when they are faced with very challenging behaviour (Selwyn *et al*, 2014). Parents want the best for their children and value targeted and timely support to help them overcome or manage difficulties. Other families may reach crisis point and feel that they have to let one child leave their family in order to protect and support his or her siblings. Families don't choose disruption but rather they reach a point where they feel that they have exhausted their coping mechanisms, run out of options, or that help has simply not been available when they and their children have desperately needed it.

Earlier editions of this guide rightly stressed the need for practical support, including domestic help; however, this continues to be a huge issue and often an "unmet" need for many families adopting brothers and sisters. Providing domestic help in the home may not only prevent parents from becoming exhausted and feeling less able to manage but can also allow them to spend more time having fun and developing relationships with their children. Sometimes extended family members and/or friends may be prepared to offer this support, freeing the adopters to focus more easily on the children's needs. However, this cannot and should not be assumed; instead, it needs to be fully explored. Most families will probably need a blend of within-family support supplemented by additional help provided by the local authority. Peer support from experienced sibling adopters is also valued highly by families and should be more routinely available to parents at different stages in their adoption journey rather than primarily or solely confined to preparation.

Adopters of sibling groups also tell us that they need much more help in managing difficult behaviours, including conflicts between their children. This is identified as a largely unmet need.

HELPING BIRTH CHILDREN AND PLACED CHILDREN TO GET ALONG

Families who already have children experience the adoption process as being focused almost exclusively on the adopted children, at the expense of other children in the family (Meakings *et al*, 2017b, p1796); in this study, adopters wanted social workers to offer more support to help children get on better. Based on their findings, the authors stressed that:

> *The decision to keep together, separate or create sibling relationships through adoption should be viewed as the start of a process of family formation, reformation or consolidation, and one which requires ongoing support for all siblings and the adopted family.*

The Child Welfare Information Gateway (2013) produced a helpful overview of *Sibling Issues in Foster Care and Adoption* (available online at www.childwelfare.gov/pubs/siblingissues/index.cfm). This cites a resource by James (2009) that sets out some strategies for parents and workers in addressing the needs of all the children in the family:

- Encourage children to share their thoughts and feelings; empathise with and do not minimise their concerns.

- Provide opportunities for fun and positive interactions between children to promote attachment.

- Promote reciprocity between children in the family; for example, if a child destroys the property of another, find a way for the child to make up for the loss.

- Find ways for parents to have meaningful individual time with each child.

- Teach children skills to resolve their own disputes as far as possible.

- Develop a support group for siblings, either informally or through an agency.

- Seek professional help for serious sibling conflicts.

RESEARCH ON POST-PLACEMENT SUPPORT

Saunders and Selwyn (2010, p7) reviewed the support needs of families who adopted a group of three or more siblings. The importance of practical support was highlighted alongside that provided through peer adopters and social workers:

- Just under half of the adopters received a high enough allowance to enable one parent to stay at home, even though staff recognised that this was important.

- Local authorities were sometimes willing to pay for a house extension or a larger car for sibling group adopters, but often adopters were expected to have a large enough home and car already.

- Agencies expected most support to come from family and friends, even though many adopters felt unable or unwilling to rely on these sources for day-to-day support.

- Adopters particularly appreciated being put in touch with other sibling group adopters.

- Local authorities were very reluctant to provide home help, even though this was really wanted by adopters who were often exhausted by basic domestic chores and wanted to spend more time with their children.

- Local authorities were also reluctant to provide respite care, except as a last resort when placements were about to disrupt.

- Most of the support given to adopters came from social workers. Adopters especially welcomed targeted help to understand things from the children's perspective, provide explanations based on children's past experiences; advocate on their behalf with other agencies; and manage difficult behaviour.

- Some social workers were highly skilled at devising strategies for helping children with attachment difficulties to feel more secure, e.g. using visual timetables to reinforce routines.

- Almost half of the adopters reported that at least one of their children had received therapy but getting this had often been difficult.

- Education was an issue for many, as teaching staff often lacked knowledge and experience of adoption and attachment issues.

Neil *et al* (2018) identified that the most frequently wanted services by all adopters (but those never received by them) were:

- life story work;

- therapeutic parenting training;

- psychological support;

- support around contact with birth family;
- counselling;
- holiday clubs/activities for children with disabilities;
- conduct problem therapies;
- cognitive and behaviour therapies;
- therapeutic camps or respite and family therapy.

ADOPTION SUPPORT FUND

The Department for Education has recognised that many adopters have struggled to access therapeutic support services that they and their children need. Consequently, the Adoption Support Fund (ASF) was set up in 2015. Adopters in England can apply for this funding through the local authority area in which they live.

Adoption support plans made at the time of the match and subsequently reviewed at LAC reviews until the adoption order is granted should consider whether there are identified therapeutic needs that can be covered by the ASF. Applications can be made for work prior to the adoption order and adopters may be reassured to know that funding is already in place. The placing local authority will be responsible for making any application to the ASF for the first three years post-adoption order, having completed an assessment of the adoption support needs. If there are identified needs for siblings beyond that time, there should be good liaison between the placing local authority and the local authority where the family resides to ensure there is continuity of support after three years.

PLANNING SUPPORT

In a helpful case study, Carden (2015) outlined her work in preparing and assessing adopters for a sibling group of five children who had been placed in two separate foster homes. She detailed the importance of a realistic package of support from the local authority, which had included:

- social work support for the children, foster carers and adoptive couple;
- financial packages – an adoption allowance for each child until they reached 18 years – this would enable both parents to remain at home to parent the children full time;

- a home extension so that the children who needed separate bedrooms would have them;
- provision of a nine-seater car – this was issued on a loan basis and was to be replaced every three years by the local authority;
- domestic help for 15 hours a week to enable both adopters to spend time with the children rather than constantly doing housework;
- education support packages, including a funded part-time teaching assistant for one child;
- education statements, psychological assessments and premium-plus payments to the local school;
- community paediatrician involvement from the start of the placement;
- therapy agreed for a year and then reviewed;
- support for adopters' time off together, even if only for a coffee together without the children; also payments agreed to fund two of the adopters' relatives to move in so that the adopters could have two short four-day breaks each year.

Many families report difficulties accessing the support that they need, when they need it. Underestimating support, delays in receiving payments and experiencing poor transfer of responsibility from one authority to another are highlighted in one family's experience below. Adoptive parents Suzanne and Daniel reflect honestly on how challenging it is to meet both the individual and combined needs of their children.

Adoptive parents – Suzanne and Daniel

Suzanne and Daniel have adopted four siblings, the three eldest of whom are boys. The brothers came into care after living in an environment of neglect and parental drug/alcohol use and violence. The boys were aged three, two and one when they were removed from the birth family; their older sibling was also removed but subsequently placed within the wider birth family.

> *There wasn't a foster placement available at the time to take all four boys together so the boys were placed in two separate placements, George and Tom were placed together and Jack was placed with their older brother. Subsequently our daughter Mia was removed at birth due to the experiences of her brothers and the lack of parental change (the adoption plan had only been finalised within court a few months prior to her birth). Mia was placed separately and she did not meet any of her brothers until she joined our family. She has never met her older brother.*

> *We were aware that there were concerns about how Jack would attach to a female carer/mother and manage alongside his brothers. Consideration was given to whether he should be placed separately. The decision was that a placement should be sought for all of the boys together.*

Suzanne wrote about the mixed feelings that the children show – wanting to be together but finding it especially hard to share her time and attention. The brothers all have some difficulties in managing their emotions, which has led to anger and some aggressive outbursts, particularly from one child:

> *After the initial delight of being together, the boys started to compete for attention and it has become apparent that their relationship is very complex. George in particular finds it very difficult to share me with the others; he loves Mia and is more understanding and accommodating with her. When he was younger he could become aggressive at times, and this increased with intensity and frequency over the past two years. His anger is mainly focused on me, and does not occur when any other adult is present, and at times towards his siblings to get a response from me.*

> *All of our children can recognise one another's distress; although she is the youngest, Mia is very good at reassuring them and comforting them. The boys are able to do this at times but only when they are feeling content. Otherwise they may compete and start to misbehave to bring the attention back to them. It feels like no matter what we do, we can never give George enough to fill him up with love. When playing together, they struggle to manage competitiveness and this is not always pleasant. They manage better when they are in twos rather than three or all four together and on the whole, play outside is more constructive.*

> *They will do things deliberately to get one another into trouble and cannot admit to things when they are in the wrong or make a wrong decision. They can be dangerous in the car, which is particularly worrying and Daniel and I have had things thrown at us by George (and on the rare occasion Tom) when we are driving. On their own they are a delight, although George is overwhelming at these times and constantly asks questions without waiting for the answer.*

I asked Suzanne and Daniel about their needs as a family and the support that they had received. Although they received some initial support and training which was helpful, there were also significant gaps. The frustration of not receiving some previously agreed payments for child care understandably left them feeling upset. However, three years post-placement, planning for the transfer of local authority responsibility and the lack of ownership within their home authority was, in their words, 'a shambles':

> *Due to the size and complexities of our family, we have accessed support from the Adoption Support Team. We were initially involved with a local*

authority outside of where we live. They provided two separate training courses for us which were great and they helped with day-to-day things as well as meeting other families in our situation. They also gave us financial support for child care when the children were young and in nursery and also during holiday times during particular periods of stress. However, almost a year later, we are still waiting to be reimbursed for child care from August 2017 and without having the fight in us we would never receive this.

Since we have transferred to our local area, the support available is very slim. During every contact that we have with the team we have been told that they don't have the resources to finance anything (we have not been asking for anything to be paid for by them). The transfer was an absolute shambles as our allocated worker was off sick. It was a very stressful time for our family as one of our sons was making the transition to a different school and his behaviour had become very aggressive towards me and we were worried that it was going to break down. No one wanted to take responsibility and we were not even offered a visit by our local team.

We had asked for therapeutic support for the family in April 2016 and this had not happened. During our initial contact with the local team (all by email), we were told not to expect a quick fix, which really upset us as we had been asking for help for so long and were told that if we did think it was going to break down, that we would be referred to the local field work team. This really angered me as adoption workers should be the most qualified people within the profession. The field work teams are often made up of newly qualified workers and they are so busy dealing with high child protection cases – what support would we get from them? Again, they did not offer to visit us. We decided that only we could get through this as a family and so we did what we could and used extra school activities to reduce some of the stress, and friends helped with the kids at times.

We also found a therapist who had experience of working with adoptive families and started to work with her. The local team has since applied for funding from the Adoption Support Fund and this has now started (after asking for it two years ago); this is going really well so far.

My husband and I have recently reflected on the support that we have received from both of the local authorities that we have been involved with. We both believe that if it hadn't been for the first team offering us financial support with things like child care, things may have broken down. Especially in the early stages when our daughter joined us, we had four children under five (our eldest son had just turned five), so some extra nursery time made a massive difference to our family.

We are often asked by professionals working with us what time my husband and I get to spend together without our children. The answer is none. We do not live close to family members and we could not just leave them with a regular babysitter due to their complex needs. We have asked both teams if there were any foster carers that they knew who could provide any support and assistance with babysitting. Our reason is that they would have a knowledge of the complexities of our children and would hopefully know how to handle things if they became distressed. Our local team stated that the local volunteer centre offered babysitting services but that it was £12 per hour. We do not have the money to spend £36 on child care on top of what it would cost us to go out for the evening.

Suzanne and Daniel suggested the following additional ideas for support that would, they think, benefit other sibling adopters:

- *Mentors as befrienders for the kids. We asked social care for this: as we have such a large family, we thought that it would be useful for our older children to have someone just for them.*

- *Being put in contact with another adoptive family who were more settled would be useful.*

- *A volunteer service to provide practical support – although we don't get the violence every day, it would be good to have someone to call for help when needed.*

As experienced children's social workers as well as being adoptive parents, Suzanne and Daniel were well aware of the importance of helping children develop emotional regulation. They wrote about how they: *name feelings with the children and try to help them understand and deal with their emotions. We are now receiving therapeutic support to assist with this. We are very open about their adoption and speak about their birth family.*

In common with many other adopters, they recognise that their children's life story books are crucially important to them. Paying attention to the quality of life story books really matters. Adopters have reported mixed experiences and highlight the importance of explanations that are fair and balanced, based on what actually happened. In the absence of this, children may harbour unrealistic fantasies about parents. Suzanne and Daniel wrote about the importance of social workers being receptive when asked to correct factual inaccuracies:

> *Their life story books are easily accessible to them and they can get them out whenever they like. The books are generally lovely but there are a number of errors in them, including where one of our children was born. When we ask for corrections to be made, we were made to feel like we were being petty and told that they were sorry that we "felt" that they were not right. We did not receive the later life letters for over a year for the boys and when we did they were again incorrect; these have never been updated as the worker has now left.*

Tips for professionals – Suzanne offered these suggestions:

- *Show empathy and compassion. Treat every family as individuals; you may have done this 100 times and have seen lots of things but for that family they are probably dealing with these things for the first time.*

- *Get paperwork correct and don't get defensive if an adopter says it's incorrect or doesn't match other information they have had. It's important to spell children's names right! Don't belittle or minimise people's experiences.*

- *Don't phone a family of young children at 4pm in the afternoon.*

- *Speak to people about attachment working both ways and reassure them that it may take time and happen with different children at different speeds. I had to fake it initially but I think that helped us all in the long term. Find out more about post-adoption depression and speak to families about it.*

Involve family and friends in the assessment and support package. We need their help and support.

The following key elements should be considered when planning support:

- **Financial support** is almost certain to be needed. Adoption allowances can be paid (subject to the required means test) when siblings are being placed together and also when a single child is joining siblings who are already placed. The costs of pre-school provision and support during school holidays are also important to address early on.

- **A settling-in grant** for equipment such as beds, a larger washing machine, etc, will also probably be needed.

- **Domestic help** could be provided in the early stages of a placement and subsequently if needed – help with washing, ironing, cleaning bedrooms, etc, can also be a good investment for larger families.

- **Transport** is an issue and a family who will have more than three children (including any they already have) will need a larger than average car, for which financial help may be necessary.

- **Housing** will be an issue for some families. Some local authorities have made a loan or grant to enable an extension to be built or to facilitate a house move. The legal department in one agency wrote to the family's building society, guaranteeing that their income, which consisted largely of adoption allowances, would not fall below the current level for X years, thus enabling the building society to make a loan. Another local authority made a loan to a family enabling an extension to be built. An agreement was drawn up stating that it need not be repaid provided the children were still in placement after 10 years. These arrangements need careful thought and planning and it is vital that they are not left to the last minute.

- **Therapeutic help** may also be needed and this too needs to be thought about and planned. For one family, a package of help and support was set up with the local Children and Adolescent Mental Health Service (CAMHS). The adopters have monthly consultation sessions that help them to support and work with their children. Should the children need individual or group therapy, there is a guarantee that this will be offered. Another family has funding agreed and access to art and music therapy for three of their children.

- **Help with managing emotions** – problems with dysregulation and emotional well-being are common in placed children and impact on behaviour, self-esteem, peer relationships and other aspects of day-to-day life. It will be important to think about each child's needs and how this affects them and might impact on family life.

- **Specific help and support with sibling behaviours and relationships** may be needed for the new family – such as managing conflict and promoting pro-social behaviour between children. It is important to focus on these aspects early on as, left unmanaged, aggressive behaviours are likely to continue and may escalate, risking placement vulnerability/breakdown. Relationship issues may involve the placed sibling group and also any existing children in the family. Research (Rushton *et al*, 2001; Selwyn *et al*, 2014) indicates that sibling relationship difficulties are a factor in less stable placements and that it is crucial that appropriate support and funding for specialist help are available when necessary.

SUMMARY

Research, practice experience and feedback from adopters are clear in conveying the importance of post-placement support. Good support packages for families are absolutely essential if they are to parent large sibling groups. However, it is clearly not just about the number of children, but the demands presented. A sibling group of two children may have wide-ranging and complex needs so their adopters may require extensive support. A comprehensive package of practical and emotional support will usually be needed, especially in the early days. The link between practical support and building attachments needs to be understood. Exhausted parents will be less emotionally available to children. Money and resources invested well can help promote relationships and placement stability.

KEY PRACTICE POINTS

- Promoting relationships between brothers and sisters is central to adoption practice whether or not siblings are placed together. Recruitment, preparation, assessment and support should ensure that the needs of brothers and sisters are embedded in policies and practice.

- There are significant links between the quality of sibling and peer relationships, for example, sibling bullying is highly correlated with bullying of peers (see Chapter 2).

- Difficulties within peer relationships are often linked with increased difficulties for children in education settings.

- Adopters want more help with managing and promoting warm, supportive sibling relationships and reducing difficult behaviour, such as conflict. These services need to be developed to help children and families early on but are also important to minimise the risk of longer-term difficulties.

- It is important to think about the "cumulative load" that may arise when caring for two or more children who have high levels of emotional and behavioural needs. Research by Selwyn *et al* (2014) suggested that it was the number of siblings with difficulties (rather than the severity of an individual child's difficulties) that was associated with the placement being rated as having major difficulties.

- Support plans must carefully address the needs of each child and the dynamics of placing particular children together. Practical and emotional impacts on the adopters should be addressed early on and reviewed.

Conclusions

Brothers and sisters have potentially the longest lasting and one of the closest relationships of their lives with each other. These relationships have enormous capacity for shared understanding, care and joy, which can help to sustain children and adults through distressing times. Even when brothers and sisters have never lived together, the significance of the relationship may be keenly felt during childhood with a sense of "what might have been" stretching into adult life.

Early planning

When children become looked after, vital decisions have to be made. Early decisions, whether based on assessment or driven by a lack of foster care resources, will have far-reaching consequences for those children involved. Planning and service provision should be informed by an understanding of sibling relationships and needs. Decisions about placement together or not in foster care and beyond, as well as the ways in which contact between separated siblings is nurtured, all have huge impact on children. When siblings are separated, visiting one another's foster home and sometimes having an overnight visit should be the norm unless there are clear safeguarding reasons.

Relationships matter

Relationships are the "golden thread" in children's lives. Children and young people themselves tell us that their relationships with brothers and sisters are crucially important to them. They want us to pay more attention to this. They want to be placed together if possible. If they cannot live together, they need to know why and they want us to make sure that visits and contact happen. Constructive working relationships established early on between foster carers looking after separated siblings can help children directly but also, and importantly so, can inform assessments.

The impact of individual experiences: shared and non-shared factors

The context of each child's experiences and history, including whether adults have shaped and reinforced patterns of interaction, or valued one child over another, will always be crucial to understand. In particular, differential treatment and different levels of affection shown by parents have consequences for how each child perceives and treats their brothers and sisters.

Working together

Foster carers and social workers have distinct and crucial roles in helping children. The ways in which foster carers are prepared generally and specifically to meet the needs of brothers and sisters is key. Understanding, or a lack of understanding, of how sibling relationships may be affected by adversity, abuse, neglect and separation will influence how foster carers respond, for example, when faced with children who may show challenging behaviours, distress or apparent indifference.

Interventions and support

Children, and their foster carers and adopters, need more help in managing troubled relationships and difficult behaviours between siblings. Problematic patterns of behaviour, such as high levels of sibling conflict, are likely to "spill over" into relationships with others. Children who show very domineering behaviour towards brothers and sisters at home may behave similarly in other settings such as nursery and school. Sibling bullying and bullying of peers are highly correlated. Young children who are physically aggressive do not just grow out of this behaviour. Service provision and interventions should develop in order to better address these and related aspects.

Links between friendships and sibling relationships

Sibling relationships provide a context for learning about "how other people tick". Many children may not have learned the skills for emotional reciprocity, and carers as well as adopters report that this can be a significant difficulty for children. Children's social skills make a big difference in whether they are accepted by others or not. An early focus on helping children to develop pro-social skills with brothers and sisters is likely to have important, long-lasting benefits for friendships in childhood and adult life.

Assessments for permanence

Within this guide, there is a strong emphasis on multi-sourcing information and corroborating evidence wherever possible. A collaborative approach between families, social workers and foster carers working together is at the heart of sibling assessments, as is the involvement of children themselves. Contact supervisors, health visitors and education staff will all have varying degrees of knowledge about children's sibling relationships. The guide both includes and encourages the use of semi-structured forms to collate information and observations from all those who can help social workers. A step-by-step process that draws on what has happened in the past, as well as what is happening currently, will contribute to a better understanding of the children, their experiences and sibling relationships.

Knowing what is happening, what is planned and why

Children and young people should be involved in making plans and have a developmentally appropriate understanding, so far as is possible, at each stage; for example, an older sibling needs to understand why they were not placed in the same foster home as younger ones. Sensitive work and consistent explanations should be provided and included in life story work and later life letters. Birth family, foster carers and adopters also need information to meet their particular needs so that they are best placed to understand decisions and respond to questions that children may ask in the years ahead.

Emotional readiness and transitions

Foster carers' and adoptive parents' readiness to work well together during introductions and beyond will have a profound impact. The emotional needs of the adults are important to think about and to address prior to introductions to the children beginning. It is vitally important that children's attachment needs are at the forefront during planning, introductions and when they move. Children should not be expected to lose significant, supportive relationships with foster carers and others. The maintenance of caring relationships should be viewed as supportive of attachment-building rather than a threat that might undermine adopters or the child's capacity to settle and thrive.

Adoptive parents of siblings

Most adopters feel positively about the decision to keep siblings together, but they also tell us that they need more targeted services. They describe sibling relationships as being fairly typical with highs and lows, but "constant conflict" between brothers and sisters is associated with higher rates of adoption breakdown. This conflict usually is apparent from early on in the placement. Parents described the most troubling behaviours as: physical aggression largely instigated by one child; coercion; and sexualised behaviour between siblings. Families who already have children experience the adoption process as being focused almost exclusively on the adopted children, at the expense of other children in the family. Adopters want more support to help children get on better.

Adopters, siblings and contact

Most adopters are supportive of contact between separated siblings and want help to make this happen and for it to be a good experience for all the children involved. Social work commitment, support and encouragement are valued by parents but often lacking.

Support

Research, practice experience and feedback from adopters and carers are clear in conveying the importance of post-placement support. Good support packages for families are absolutely essential if they are to parent large sibling groups. However, it is clearly not just about the number of children, but the demands presented. The links between practical support and building attachments need to be understood. Exhausted parents or carers will be less emotionally available to children. Money and resources invested well can help promote relationships and placement stability so that brothers and sisters have the best chance to succeed in life.

References

Adoption Research Initiative (2011) *Family Finding and Matching: A survey of adoption agency practice in England and Wales*, Summary 4, available online at: www.adoptionresearchinitiative.org.uk

Ahmad A and Betts B (2003) *My Life Story*, London: Interactive Resources

Ainsworth M, Blehar M, Waters E and Wall S (1978) *Patterns of Attachment: A psychological study of the strange situation*, Hillsdale, NJ: Erlbaum

Alink LR, Mesman J, van Zeiji J, Stolk MN, Juffer F, Koot HM, Bakermans-Kranenburg MJ and van IJzendoorn MH (2006) 'The early childhood aggression curve: development of physical aggression in 10- to 50-month-old children', *Child Development*, 77:4, pp 954–66

Argent H (2008) *Ten Top Tips on Placing Siblings*, London: BAAF

Ashley C and Roth D (2015) *What Happens to Siblings in the Care System?*, London: Family Rights Group

Barth R and Berry M (1988) *Modern Applications of Social Work: Adoption and disruption*, Hawthorne, NY: Aldine de Gruyter

Beckett S (2002) 'Split up but not cut off: making and sustaining contact arrangements between siblings', in Argent H (ed) *Staying Connected: Managing contact arrangements in adoption*, London: BAAF

Beckett S and Hershman D (2001) 'The human rights implications for looked after siblings', *Family Law*, April

Boddy J (2013) *Understanding Permanence for Looked After Children: A review of research for the Care Inquiry*, available online at: http://sro.sussex.ac.uk/44711/1/Boddy_2013_Understanding_Permanence.pdf

Boivin M (2014) 'Peer relations', in Tremblay RE, Boivin M and Peters RDeV (eds) *Encyclopedia on Early Childhood Development*, available online at: www.child-encyclopedia.com/sites/default/files/dossiers-complets/en/peer-relations.pdf

Boswell S and Cudmore L (2014) 'The children were fine': acknowledging the complex feelings in the move from foster care to adoption', *Adoption & Fostering*, 38:1, pp 5–21

Boyle C (2017) 'What is the impact of birth family contact on children in adoption and long-term foster care? A systematic review', *Child and Family Social Work*, 22, pp 22–33

REFERENCES

Brown L, Moore S and Turney D (2012) *Analysis and Critical Thinking in Assessment*, Dartington: Research in Practice

Buist K, Dekovic M and Prinzie P (2013) 'Sibling relationship quality and psychopathology of children and adolescents: a meta-analysis', available online at: www.researchgate.net/publication/233536695_Sibling_relationship_quality_and_psychopathology_of_children_and_adolescents_A_meta-analysis

Buist K and Vermande M (2014) 'Sibling relationship patterns and their associations with child competence and problem behaviour', *Journal of Family Psychology*, 28:4, pp 529–37

Carden M (2015) 'Assessing sibling relationships for placement: a case study', *Seen and Heard*, 25: 2, pp 26–35

Care Inquiry (2013) *Making not Breaking: Building relationships for our most vulnerable children*, available online at: www.nuffieldfoundation.org/sites/default/files/files/Care%20Inquiry%20-%20Full%20Report%20April%202013.pdf

Centres for Disease Control and Prevention, National Center for Injury Prevention and Control, and Division of Violence Prevention (2014) *The Adverse Childhood Experiences (ACE) Study*, available online at: www.cdc.gov/violenceprevention/acestudy/index.html

Centre of Excellence for Children's Well-Being (2009) *Peer Relations: Sowing the seeds of friendship*, Quebec, Canada: CECWB

Child Welfare Information Gateway (2013) *Sibling Issues in Foster Care and Adoption*, available online at: www.childwelfare.gov/pubs/siblingissues/index.cfm

Children's Society (2015) *The Good Childhood Report 2015*, available online at: www.childrenssociety.org.uk/sites/default/files/TheGoodChildhoodReport2015.pdf

Department for Children, Schools and Families (2010) *Sufficiency: Statutory guidance on securing sufficient accommodation for looked after children*, available online at: https://assets.publishing.service.gov.uk/government/uploads/system/uploads/attachment_data/file/273812/sufficiency_-_statutory_guidance_on_securing_sufficient_accommodation_for_looked_after_children.pdf

Department for Education (2011) *Putting Care into Practice: Training programme for the revised legal framework for looked after children*, London: DfE

Department for Education (2013) *Statutory Guidance on Adoption*, London: DfE

Department for Education (2018a) *Fostering Better Outcomes: The Government response to the Education Select Committee report into fostering and foster care in England*, available online at: www.gov.uk/government/publications/fostering-better-outcomes

Department for Education (2018b) *Working Together to Safeguard Children: A guide to inter-agency working to safeguard and promote the welfare of children,* available online at: https://assets.publishing.service.gov.uk/government/uploads/system/uploads/attachment_data/file/722305/Working_Together_to_Safeguard_Children_-_Guide.pdf

Department for Education and Department of Health (2015) *Promoting the Health and Well-Being of Looked-After Children: Statutory guidance for local authorities, CCGs and NHS England*, London: DfE

Department of Health (1991) *Patterns and Outcomes in Child Placement: Messages from current research and their implications*, London: DH

Dibben E with Butcher L and Upright H (2018) *Think Siblings Project: Messages for practice when assessing the needs of siblings for permanent placement and supporting siblings in adoptive families*, available online at: www.coram.org.uk/thinksiblings

Dunbar L (2009) *Ten Top Tips for Making Introductions*, London: BAAF

Family Futures (2007, updated 2019) *Assessing Sibling Placements, Practice Paper*, available at: www.familyfutures.co.uk/wp-content/uploads/2019/06/Practice-Paper-Siblings-June-2019.pdf

Family Justice Review Panel (2011) *Family Justice Review: Final report*, available online at: https://assets.publishing.service.gov.uk/government/uploads/system/uploads/attachment_data/file/217343/family-justice-review-final-report.pdf

Farnfield S (2009) 'A modified Strange Situation procedure for use in assessing sibling relationships and their attachment to carers', *Adoption & Fostering*, 33:1, pp 4–17

Featherstone B, Gupta A and Mills S (2018) *The Role of the Social Worker in Adoption: Ethics and human rights – an enquiry*, Birmingham: BASW, available online at: www.basw.co.uk/adoption-enquiry

Feinberg ME, Solmeyer AR and McHale SM (2012) 'The third rail of family systems: sibling relationships, mental and behavioural health, and preventive intervention in childhood and adolescence', *Clinical Child and Family Psychology Review*, 15:1, pp 43–57

Fortuna K, Goldner I and Knafo A (2010) 'Twin relationships: a comparison across monozygotic twins, dizygotic twins and nontwin siblings in early childhood', *Family Science*, 1:3–4, pp 205–211

Furman W and Buhrmester D (1985) 'Children's perceptions of the qualities of sibling relationships', *Child Development*, 56:2, pp 448–61

REFERENCES

Goodman R (1997) 'The Strengths and Difficulties Questionnaire', *Journal of Child Psychology and Psychiatry*, 38:5, pp 581–86

Groza V, Maschmeier C, Jamison C and Piccola T (2003) 'Siblings and out-of-home placement: best practices', *Families in Society*, 84:4, pp 480–490

Hadley Centre for Adoption and Foster Care Studies and Coram Voice (2015) *Children and Young People's Views on Being in Care: A literature review*, London: Hadley Centre and Coram Voice

Hammond S and Cooper N (2013) *Digital Life Story Work: Using technology to help young people make sense of their experiences*, London: BAAF

Hasting R (2013) *Children and Adolescents who are the Siblings of Children with Intellectual Disabilities or Autism*, Warwick: University of Warwick

Hegar R (2005) 'Sibling placement in foster care and adoption: an overview of international research', *Children and Youth Services Review*, 27, pp 717–39

Herrick M and Piccus W (2005) 'Sibling connections: the importance of nurturing sibling bonds in the foster care system', *Children and Youth Services Review*, 27:7, pp 845–61

Howe D (1998) *Patterns of Adoption*, London: Blackwell Science

Howe N, Della Porta S, Recchia H, Funamoto A and Ross H (2015) '"This bird can't do it 'cause this bird doesn't swim in water": sibling teaching during naturalistic home observations in early childhood', *Journal of Cognition and Development*, 16, pp 314–32

Howe N and Recchia H (2014) *Sibling Relations and their Impact on Children's Development*, Toronto: Concordia University, Canada

Iyer P, Boddy J, Hammelsbeck R and Lynch-Huggins S (2020) *Contact following Placement in Care, Adoption, or Special Guardianship: Implications for children and young people's well-being*, Evidence Review, London: Nuffield Family Justice Observatory

James A (2009) *Brothers and Sisters in Adoption: Helping children navigate relationships when new kids join the family*, New York, NY: Perspectives

James S, Monn A, Palinkas L and Leslie L (2008) 'Maintaining sibling relationships for children in foster and adoptive placements', *Children and Youth Services Review*, 30, pp 90–106

Jones C and Henderson G (2017) *Supporting Sibling Relationships of Children in Permanent Fostering and Adoptive Families*, Research Briefing 1, Strathclyde: University of Strathclyde

Kalvin C, Bierman K and Erath S (2015) *Prevention and Intervention Programs Promoting Positive Peer Relations in Early Childhood*, available online at: www.child-encyclopedia.com/sites/default/files/textes-experts/en/829/prevention-and-intervention-programs-promoting-positive-peer-relations-in-early-childhood.pdf

Kenyon P and Forde E (2020) 'Thousands of siblings split up in care system', BBC News, 14 January, available at: www.bbc.co.uk/news/uk-51095939

Kosonen M (1996) 'Maintaining sibling relationships – neglected dimension in child care practice', *British Journal of Social Work*, 26, pp 809–822

Kosonen M (1999) '"Core" and kin siblings: foster children's changing families', in Mullender A (ed) *We are Family: Sibling relationships in placement and beyond*, London: BAAF, pp 28–49

Kothari B, Sorenson P, McBeath B and Steele J (2017) 'An intervention to improve sibling relationship quality among youth in foster care: results of a randomised clinical trial', *Child Abuse and Neglect*, 63, pp 19–29

Kramer L (2010) 'The essential ingredients of successful sibling relationships: an emerging framework for advancing theory and practice', *Child Development Perspectives*, 4, pp 87–94

Leathers S (2005) 'Separation from siblings: associations with placement adaptation and outcomes among adolescents in long-term foster care', *Children and Youth Services Review*, 27, pp 793–819

Lereya ST, Samara M and Wolke D (2013) 'Parenting behaviour and the risk of becoming a victim and a bully/victim: a meta-analysis study', *Child Abuse & Neglect*, 37:12, pp 1091–1108

Linares L, Jimenez J, Nesci C, Pearson E, Beller S, Edwards N and Levin-Rector A (2015) 'Reducing sibling conflict in maltreated children placed in foster homes', *Prevention Science*, 39, pp 1–10

Lord J and Borthwick S (2008) *Together or Apart: Assessing siblings for permanent placement*, London: BAAF

Macaskill C (2002) *Safe Contact: Children in permanent placements and contact with their birth relatives*, London: Russell House

McBeath B, Kothari B, Blakeslee J, Lamson-Siu E, Bank L, Linares LO, Waid J, Sorenson P, Jimenez J, Pearson E and Shlonsky A (2014) 'Intervening to improve outcomes for siblings in foster care: conceptual, substantive, and methodological dimensions of a prevention science framework', *Child Youth Services Review*, 39:1 pp 1–10

McGuire S, Updegraff K and McHale S (1996) 'Children's perceptions of the sibling relationship in middle childhood: connections within and between family relationships', *Personal Relationships*, 3:3, pp 229–39

McHale S, Kimberly A, Updegraff K and Whiteman S (2012) 'Sibling relationships and influences in childhood and adolescence', *Journal of Marriage and the Family*, 74:5, pp 913–930

Meakings S, Coffey A and Shelton K (2017a) 'The influence of adoption on sibling relationships: experiences and support needs of newly formed adoptive families', *British Journal of Social Work*, 47:6, pp 1781–1799

Meakings S, Sebba J and Luke N (2017b) *What is Known about the Placement and Outcomes of Siblings in Foster Care? An international literature review*, London: Rees Centre, University of Oxford and DfE

Meakings S, Ottaway H, Doughty J, Coffey A and Shelton K (2018) 'The support needs and experiences of newly formed adoptive families: findings from the Wales Adoption Study', *Adoption & Fostering*, 42:1, pp 58–75

Milich L, Goulder S and Gibson S (2017) *Improving Mental Health Support for our Children and Young People*, London: SCIE

Monk D and Macvarish J (2018) *Siblings, Contact and the Law: An overlooked relationship? Summary report*, Nuffield Foundation, available at: www.nuffieldfoundation.org/wp-content/uploads/2019/11/Final20Siblings20Summary.pdf

Monk D and Macvarish J (2020) *Brothers and Sisters in Public Law Proceedings: Assessment, placement, permanence and contact, Research in Practice Frontline Briefing*, London: Research in Practice

Morgan R (2009) *Keeping in Touch: A report of children's experience by the Children's Rights Director for England*, London: Ofsted

Mullender A (ed) (1999) *We are Family: Sibling relationships in placement and beyond*, London: BAAF

National Recruitment Forum (2013) *Improving Practice on the Placement of Siblings for Adoption*, London: NRF

National Scientific Council on the Developing Child (2010) *Persistent Fear and Anxiety can Affect Young Children's Learning and Development*, Working Paper No. 9, available online at: www.developingchild.net

Neil E, Beek M and Schofield G (2020) *The UEA Moving to Adoption Model: A guide for adoption social workers, fostering social workers and children's social workers*, Norwich: University of East Anglia, Centre for Research on Children and Families

Neil E, Beek M and Ward E (2013) *Contact after Adoption: A follow up in late adolescence*, available online at: www.uea.ac.uk/documents/3437903/0/Contact+report+NEIL+dec+20+v2+2013.pdf/f2d766c7-39eb-49a3-93b7-1f1368a071a1

Neil E, Beek M and Ward E (2015) *Contact after Adoption: A longitudinal study of post-adoption contact arrangements*, London: BAAF

Neil E, Copson R and Sorensen P (2020) *Contact during Lockdown: How are children and their birth families keeping in touch?*, Briefing Paper, London: Nuffield Family Justice Observatory/UEA

Neil E, Young J and Hartley L (2018) *The Joys and Challenges of Adoptive Family Life: A survey of adoptive parents in the Yorkshire and Humberside region*, Norwich: UEA

NICE (2010, updated 2015) *Looked-After Children and Young People*, Public Health Guideline 28, London: NICE

Ofsted (2015) *National Statistics, Fostering in England*, London: Ofsted

Panksepp J (1998) *Affective Neuroscience: The foundations of human and animal emotions*, Oxford: Oxford University Press

Pike A, Kretschmer T and Dunn J (2009) 'Siblings: friends or foes?', *The Psychologist*, 494–96

Rees J (2017) *Life Story Books for Adopted and Fostered Children*, London: Jessica Kingsley Publishers

Richardson S and Yates TM (2014) 'Siblings in foster care: a relational path to resilience', *Children and Youth Services Review*, 47, pp 378–388

Ross T (2017) *My Book of Feelings, A Book to Help Children with Attachment Difficulties, Learning or Developmental Disabilities Understand their Emotions*, London: Jessica Kingsley Publishers

Rushton A, Dance C, Quinton D and Mayes D (2001) *Siblings in Late Permanent Placements*, London: BAAF

Ryan M (2020) *Contact between Children in Care or Adopted and their Families: Six key messages from research*, Briefing Paper, Nuffield Family Justice Observatory, available at: www.nuffieldfjo.org.uk/app/nuffield/files-module/local/documents/contact-six-key-messages-nuffieldfjo.pdf

Samek DR and Rueter MA (2011) 'Associations between family communication patterns, sibling closeness, and adoptive status', *Journal of Marriage and the Family*, 73:5, pp 1015–1031

Sattler K, Font S and Gershoff E (2018) 'Age-specific risk factors associated with placement instability among foster children', *Child Abuse & Neglect*, 84: October, pp. 157–169

Saunders H and Selwyn J (2010) *Adopting Large Sibling Groups: The experiences of agencies and adopters in placing sibling groups for adoption from care*, London: Hadley Centre

Saunders H, Selwyn J and Fursland E (2013) *Placing Large Sibling Groups for Adoption*, London: BAAF

REFERENCES

SCIE (2008) *Communication Skills: E-learning course*, available at: www.scie.org.uk/e-learning/communication-skills

SCIE (2010) *Promoting the Quality of Life of Looked-After Children and Young People*, London: SCIE

Schofield G and Beek M (2018) *The Attachment Handbook for Foster Care and Adoption* (2nd edn), London: CoramBAAF

Sebba J (2017) *Evaluation of the Siblings Together Buddy Project: Final report*, available online at: http://reescentre.education.ox.ac.uk/wordpress/wp-content/uploads/2017/04/evaluation_siblingstogether_reescentreapril2017.pdf

Segal N (2012) *Born Together – Reared Apart: The Landmark Minnesota Twin Study*, Cambridge, MA: Harvard University Press

Selwyn J (2004) 'Placing older children in new families: changing patterns of contact', in Neil E and Howe D (eds) *Contact in Adoption and Permanent Foster Care*, London: BAAF, pp 144–164

Selwyn J (2017) *Post-Adoption Support and Interventions for Adoptive Families: Best practice approaches*, Munich: Deutches Jugendinstitut

Selwyn J (2018) 'Sibling relationships in adoptive families that disrupted or were in crisis', *Research on Social Work Practice*, 1:11

Selwyn J and Briheim-Crookall L (2017) *Our Lives, Our Care: Looked after children's views on their well-being*, Bristol: University of Bristol

Selwyn J, Magnus L and Stuijfzand B (2018) *Our Lives, Our Care: Looked after children's views on their well-being in 2017*, available online at: https://coramvoice.org.uk/sites/default/files/1053-CV-Our-Lives-Our-Care-report5.pdf

Selwyn J, Wijedasa D and Meakings S (2014) *Beyond the Adoption Order: Challenges, interventions and adoption disruption*, London: BAAF

Selwyn J and Wood M (2015) *Measuring Wellbeing: A literature review*, Bristol: University of Bristol

Shemmings D (2016) 'Never use the word "attachment" again', *Community Care*, 9 August, available at: www.communitycare.co.uk/2016/08/09/never-use-word-attachment/

Shemmings D (2018) 'Why social workers shouldn't use "attachment" in their records and reports', *Community Care*, 28 June, available at: www.communitycare.co.uk/2018/06/28/social-workers-shouldnt-use-attachment-records-reports/

Shlonsky A, Elkins J, Bellamy J and Ashare C (2005) 'The other kin: setting the course for research, policy and practice with siblings in foster care', *Children and Youth Services Review*, 27, pp 697–716

Teicher MH and Vitaliano GD (2011) 'Witnessing violence toward siblings: an understudied but potent form of early adversity', *Plus One*, 6:12

Thoburn J (2018) 'Research on the birth family contact for children who need out-of-home care', *Seen and Heard*, 28:3

Thomas C (2012) *Adoption for Looked After Children*, London: BAAF

Trembley RE, Boivin M and Peters RDeV (eds) (2014) *Encyclopedia on Early Childhood Development*, available online at: www.child-encyclopedia.com/sites/default/files/dossiers-complets/en/peer-relations.pdf

Tucker C, Jenkins C, McHale S and Crouter A (2008) 'Links between older and younger adolescent siblings' adjustment: the moderating role of shared activities', *International Journal of Behavioural Development*, 32:2, pp152–60

Waid J, Kothari B, Dahlgren J and McBeath B (2021) 'Exploring mechanisms of change in a dyadic relationship intervention for siblings in foster care', *Child & Family Social Work*, doi: 10.1111/cfs.12833

Waid J and Wojciak A (2017) 'Evaluation of a multi-site program designed to strengthen relational bonds for siblings separated by foster care', *Evaluation and Program Planning*, 64, pp 69–77

Watson D, Latter S and Bellew R (2015) 'Adopted children's and young people's views on their life storybooks: the role of narrative in the formation of identities', *Children and Youth Services Review*, 58, pp 90–98

Weld N and Greening M (2004) 'The Three Houses', *Social Work Now*, 29, pp 34–37

Whincup H (2010) *Involving Children in Assessment and Decision-Making*, Stirling: University of Stirling

Wojciak A, Helfrich C and Mcwey L (2013) 'Sibling relationships on internalising symptoms of youth in foster care', *Children and Youth Services Review*, 35:7, pp 1071–77

Wolke D, Tippett N and Dantchev S (2015) 'Bullying in the family: sibling bullying', *The Lancet Psychiatry*, 2, pp 917–29

Appendices

Appendix 1: Overview of legislation, guidance and NICE and SCIE guidance	**158**
Appendix 2: Forms and sample letters	**167**
Foster carers – Initial overview for each child	167
Contact supervisor – Observations of contact: interactions during family contact with parents and between siblings	168
Foster carers – Observations of contact: contact between separated siblings	170
Foster carers – Observations of sibling relationships: positive and negative aspects	172
Children's physical aggression towards others (handout for foster carers)	176
Foster carers – Identifying difficult patterns of behaviour and aggression	177
Parents and relatives – Views about the children and their sibling relationships	179
Parents and relatives – Exploring siblings' roles and any differential treatment of children	181
Sibling assessment: key elements (for social workers)	183
Education – Observations of child (pre-school and school)	184
Observations by health staff	187
Appendix 3: Useful reading and online resources	**189**
Appendix 4: Adopters' accounts	**193**

FORMS AVAILABLE FOR PURCHASE

The forms and sample letters in Appendix 2 are available here for agencies to copy, amend and use as they wish. All of these forms and sample letters are also available as Word templates for purchase; the set of forms costs £25.00 plus VAT = £30.00. These can be purchased, for unlimited future use, at: www.corambaaf.org.uk/bookshop, or by contacting CoramBAAF Publications Sales at pubs.sales@corambaaf.org.uk or on 020 7520 7517.

Appendix 1
Overview of legislation, guidance and NICE and SCIE guidance

Below is a summary of relevant law and guidance in the UK, as it pertains to the placement of siblings and contact between them, and relevant NICE/SCIE guidance, followed by a selection of case law.

WHAT DOES THE LAW SAY?

The law and guidance in the UK are clear that siblings should be placed together if possible and consistent with their welfare, and that contact between siblings should be considered should one or more of them be looked after and placed separately from others.

The **Children Act 1989** was the first piece of British child care legislation to specifically refer to siblings and their placement. This placed a duty on local authorities, so far as reasonably practicable, to place siblings together. This is based on a clear presumption that, subject to welfare considerations, this would generally be the best option for children.

> *The local authority must ensure that the placement is such that ... if C has a sibling for whom the local authority are also providing accommodation, it enables C and the sibling to live together.*
>
> (s.22c(8)(c) Children Act 1989, duplicated in s.81(8)(c) Social Services and Wellbeing (Wales) Act 2014, and Art.27(8)(b) Children (Northern Ireland) (Order) 1995)

It should, however, be noted that this duty is disapplied in England and Wales if the local authority is placing a child in an early permanence placement.

In Scotland, a similar duty is contained in Reg 4(5) of the Looked After Children (Scotland) Regulations 2009, with the additional requirement that, if siblings are not placed in the same foster or residential home, they should be placed in homes as near together as appropriate and practicable. The Regulation does not use the term sibling, but refers to "children in the same family" to reflect that children can live in complex family units and it is their perceived relationship with other children that must be considered, not just a legal or biological connection.

Schedule 2 para 15(1)c of the Children Act 1989, Art. 29 of the Children (Northern Ireland) Order 1995, and s.95 of the Social Services and Wellbeing (Wales) Act 2014 stipulate that:

> Where a child is being looked after by a local authority, the authority shall, unless it is not reasonably practicable or consistent with his welfare, endeavour to promote contact between the child and... c) any relative, friend or other person connected with him.

The definition of "relative" includes brothers and sisters (s.105(1) Children Act 1989, Art. 2 Children (Northern Ireland) Order 1995, s.197(1) Social Services and Wellbeing (Wales) Act 2014).

Schedule 7 to the Children Act 1989, Sch 5 of the Children (Northern Ireland) Order and Reg 27A of the Looked After Children (Scotland) Regulations 2009 prohibit the placement of more than three children with foster carers, unless a specific exemption is given. However, it recognises the importance of keeping siblings together by allowing this "usual fostering limit" to be exceeded if the children are all members of the same sibling group.

The term "sibling" is not defined in the statutes or Regulations but is expected to be given the normal meaning of "brothers and sisters". The definitions of "relative" include those connected by full blood, half-blood or marriage or civil partnership and so siblings would include half-brothers and sisters and stepbrothers and sisters.

Section 1 of the Adoption and Children Act 2002 (England and Wales) requires the court and adoption agency, when coming to a decision relating to the adoption of a child, to have regard to 'the child's ascertainable wishes and feelings...' (considered in the light of the child's age and understanding) and 'the relationship which the child has with relatives...including...the likelihood of any such relationship continuing and the value to the child of its doing so'. The Adoption and Children (Scotland) Act 2007 requires an agency to have regard to the views of relatives when placing a child.

The Adoption Agencies Regulations for England 2005, Wales 2005, Northern Ireland 1989 and Scotland 2009 all require a child's permanence report to be written when adoption is being considered as the plan. It must include information on the child's siblings and whether they are also to be adopted. Regulations in England and Wales require the agency to address 'the likelihood of any such relationship continuing and the value to the child of its doing so', while Scotland asks the agency to consider whether it would be in the child's interests to place them together.

In all areas of the UK, the relevant adoption support or allowance regulations allow financial support to be considered where it is desirable for the child to be placed with the same adoptive parent as his or her brother or sister, whether a full or a half-sibling, or with a child with whom he or she has previously shared a home. (This includes single children joining siblings as well as siblings being placed as a group.)

Early planning: placements and contact

Sibling placements and contact

The Children Act 1989 Guidance and Regulations Volume 2: Care planning, placement and case review (as updated June 2015) and the Guidance on Looked After Children (Scotland) Regulations 2009 contain sections that are especially pertinent in respect of planning contact and making placements.

Wherever it is in the best interests of each individual child, siblings should be placed together. Being able to live with brothers and sisters where they are also looked after is described as being an important protective factor for many looked after children (3.21 and 3.23, England Guidance; also Adoption and Children Act 2002; and Reg. 4(5) Scotland Guidance).

Whilst it is not always possible or appropriate to place siblings together, guidance in England states that contact should then be actively planned to support the development of healthy relationships between brothers and sisters. Scotland guidance imposes a duty on local authorities to assess a child's need for contact with siblings. The Children (Northern Ireland) Order 1995 states that a local authority shall 'endeavour to promote contact' between the child and other relatives, including siblings.

Furthermore, guidance in England and Scotland states that children must be supported to understand why they cannot live together.

The England guidance recognises that some children will be separated on entry into care, but states at para 3.25:

> *If it is likely that brothers and sisters who are not able to be placed together at the start of a care episode will remain looked after for the medium to long term, arrangements should be made as part of each child's care plan which will enable brothers and sisters to live together, taking into account the other factors.* (s.22c(8)(b))

Scotland guidance states:

> *In terms of Regulation 4(5), local authorities should try to ensure that siblings (children in the same family) are placed together...Where this proves impossible, they should, wherever possible, be placed near each other.*

England guidance requires local authorities to take account of their local need for sibling placements. IROs should monitor the changes in need among their own caseload and should report regularly to the Corporate Parenting Board on this issue (2.86). (Also note that local authorities have a statutory responsibility under the Sufficiency Duty to ensure that a range of accommodation through a number of providers is available to meet the local demand and needs of their population of looked after children. See *Sufficiency: Statutory Guidance on Securing Sufficient Accommodation for Looked After Children* (2010).

Scotland guidance (Reg. 6) states:

> *In order to provide sufficient placements for sibling groups, a strategic approach to placement or children and the recruitment of foster carers is essential. Specific recruitment activity with a focus upon the need to keep sibling groups together may be required.*

Where siblings placed together in foster care may be separated when one turns 18, the responsible authority should consider whether "staying put" arrangements may be beneficial for all the children involved (3.23, England guidance).

England guidance (2.85) notes that maintaining contact with siblings is reported by children to be one of their highest priorities and that contact:

> *...can provide continuity and stability for a child in a time of uncertainty and possibly great change. Sibling contact can help a child maintain their identity in an unfamiliar environment and promote self-esteem and emotional support.*

Contact must be meaningful and take place where children feel safe and supported. Guidance in England, Scotland and Wales states that children's wishes and feelings about all the arrangements made for them should be ascertained, as well as the carers' views. Children should know what contact is planned and about any changes such as why contact is cancelled or does not happen (see 2.87 and 2.88, England guidance; Reg. 6, Scotland guidance).

There is a specific requirement for the care plan to set out arrangements for the promotion and maintenance of contact with brothers and sisters, so far as this is consistent with the child's welfare (Schedule 1, para 3(1), and Schedule 1, para 3(4) of the Care Planning, Placement and Case Review (England) Regulations 2010; Schedule 2, paras 3(1) and 3(4) of the Care Planning, Placement and Case Review (Wales) Regulations 2015). Where contact stops because it is against the child's wishes or best interests, contact should be regularly reviewed and children should understand that they can change their mind. Children should also be supported through problems with contact, if they wish to maintain it.

Scotland guidance (Reg. 6) states:

Where it is not in children's best interests for them to be placed together, or this has proved unachievable, then it may still be appropriate for frequent contact to be maintained...Where siblings are placed separately, reunification should be considered at the first and all subsequent reviews, particularly where separation was dictated by a shortfall of placements.

IROs should ensure that care plan review meetings consider sibling contact and should check whether the child is happy with the frequency and quality of contact that they are having. The child's views should be included in all assessments and reviews. Children should be informed that they have the same IRO as their siblings. Their IRO should advise children how they can access advocacy services if they have a complaint. IROs must also address the issue of sibling contact in their annual report (2.89 and 2.90, England guidance).

Scotland guidance (Regs 44 and 45) sets out details about child care reviews and what these should cover, including taking stock of the child's needs and taking their views into account.

Each local authority should discuss with their Children in Care Council their policy and procedures on sibling contact and review their performance. They should also consider producing guides for both children and young people about their rights and entitlements to sibling contact with their Children in Care Council and holding an annual survey of children's views on this issue (2.91, England guidance).

The National Adoption Service (NAS) in Wales recognises the need to modernise various elements of adoption practice. This includes "contact" and as a first step NAS is working with the Welsh Government to address the recommendation about sibling contact contained in the Children's Commissioner for Wales 2016-17 Annual Report.

Adoption planning

In the context of considering adoption, the Adoption and Children Act 2002 emphasised that the *lifelong implications of adoption should be considered* when planning placements and making decisions for children. Arguably, this is especially pertinent when considering separation of one or more children from other siblings, as are human rights considerations.

Human rights legislation is also relevant here (see Beckett and Hershman, *Family Law*, April 2001). Article 8 of the European Convention on Human Rights was brought into UK domestic law by the Human Rights Act 1998 – this covers the right to respect for private and family life and prohibits interference with this. Family life in this context would certainly include siblings living together. Exceptions can be made to protect "health and morals" and the "rights and freedoms of others".

This clearly allows "interference" in order to protect a child's right not to be subjected to harm by family members. Article 8 does reinforce the presumption that siblings living together should not be separated.

Note: when one child has been adopted, the legal relationship between that child and any member of their birth family is brought to an end. There will be no residual Article 8 right to a family life where there is no remaining legal connection and the siblings have not established a relationship, e.g. where one child is adopted before their sibling is born.

The then President of the Family Division, Lord Justice Munby, stated that:

The placement of a child in foster care, and the selection of a particular placement, must take into account the Article 8 rights of both the child's parents and any siblings…Any separation of siblings involves an interference with the family life of each of them, and thus has to be justified in accordance with the usual Article 8 criteria…The geographical location of a foster placement has to take into account the Article 8 rights of the parents, the siblings and members of the wider family to have contact with the child who is in care.

(VOICE National Conference, 2006)

NICE AND SCIE GUIDANCE

The extract below is taken from NICE (National Institute for Health and Care Excellence) guidance Public Health Guideline 28, *Looked-After Children and Young People* (2010, updated 2015),

3.13: The PDG (Programme Development Group) heard that a large number (up to 80%) of looked-after children and young people who have a brother or sister also in care are living separately from them. Thorough assessment is required if siblings are to be separated. The PDG took the view that placements that enable siblings to live together or close by or which allow them to attend the same school are likely to be beneficial. However, it was noted that this is not always the case and there may be situations where it is preferable to separate siblings.

The extracts below are taken from SCIE (Social Care Institute for Excellence) recommendations, *Promoting the Quality of Life of Looked-After Children and Young People* (2010).

Sibling placements and contact

Evidence suggests that membership of a sibling group is a unique part of the identity of a child or young person and can promote a sense of belonging and promote positive self-esteem and emotional wellbeing. Good management of sibling placement and contact is important to

encourage and nurture healthy relationships, and can also help children and young people manage relationships they may find difficult. Siblings can include those who are not looked after and 'sibling-like' relationships that develop in a care setting.

Recommendation 15 Support sibling placements

Who should take action?

- *Placement teams*
- *Social workers and social work managers*

What action should they take?

- *Ensure that all decisions taken about sibling care, placement and contact (including recommendations below) includes siblings who may be adopted, those who share one birth parent, and stepbrothers and stepsisters.*

- *Ensure contact orders made by a court are followed, and place siblings together unless assessments and the wishes of the child or young person suggest otherwise.*

- *Ensure a placement strategy is in place that addresses any shortage of foster carers or suitable residential placements to meet the needs of sibling groups, for example through:*
    - *recruiting foster families specifically for sibling groups;*
    - *commissioning homes for small family groups;*
    - *meeting the additional financial and housing needs of foster carers to enable siblings to be placed together.*

- *Where a looked-after child or young person has a brother or sister in care, identify a placement that allows siblings to live together unless there is clear evidence that this would not be in their best interests, or the child or young person is unhappy with the arrangement.*

- *Ensure this approach applies equally to siblings of multiple heritage. Ensure siblings have the same social worker, wherever possible and practical.*

- *Establish a clear communication and liaison plan where siblings have different social workers.*

- *Where decisions are made to separate sibling family groups:*
    - *record clearly and explain sensitively to the child or young person the reasons for separation (see also recommendations 1, 2, 7 and 24)*
    - *make robust plans for ongoing sibling contact according to the wishes of the child or young person*

- ensure social workers co-ordinate any ongoing contact desired by the child or young person, arranging appropriate supervision where necessary and supporting foster or residential carers

- review a separation decision if the circumstances of a sibling change.

- Provide additional support and resources that help the co-placement of siblings to prevent disruption and possible end of a placement for any child or young person in a sibling family group.

- Where siblings live or are placed in different local authority areas ensure that arrangements are in place for their independent reviewing officers or social workers to liaise on their needs, ensuring ongoing contact and any possibility of future co-placement are regularly considered from the perspective and wishes of each sibling (see Recommendation 24).

The key part of Recommendation 24 that relates to meeting the individual needs and preferences of looked after children and young people sets out:

Who should take action?

- Social workers and social work managers
- Independent reviewing officers

What action should they take?

- Promote continued contact with former carers, siblings or family members personally valued by the child or young person where this is felt to be in their best interests. Where this is not possible, acknowledge the significance of losing former attachment figures and relationships.

CASE LAW

The courts in England have consistently recognised the importance of a sibling relationship – even if they have not necessarily reinforced that relationship with an order.

Re R (A Child) [2005] EWCA Civ 1128: A four-year-old child was placed for adoption with the intention that she would have face-to-face contact with her 17-year-old sister three times a year. The prospective adopters then changed their views and agreed to only one contact visit per year. The older sister applied for leave to issue an application for contact. The court accepted that it would be very unusual to make a contact order against the wishes of adopters, and refused the older sister permission to apply, although they did say that they might have thought differently if the adopters had refused all contact, as the sibling relationship was one that should be preserved.

Re P-M (A Child) [2013] EWHC 1838: A child (P-M) was placed with a foster carer, Ms D, at the age of four months. After some time, the local authority approved her as an adopter for him. He had several siblings, some, including a younger sister, who were cared for by their maternal grandmother. The grandmother was unable to look after another child and supported P-M's adoption by Ms D. However, she was concerned that she and P-M's sister should have their ongoing contact with P-M secured by a contact order. Ms D assured the court that she intended contact to continue and opposed the making of an order. The court nonetheless made a limited order, including provision for the siblings to have contact with each other.

Re T (A Child: Adoption or Special Guardianship) [2017] EWCA Civ 1797: The Court of Appeal upheld the making of a placement order in respect of a child, Liam. Liam was placed with relatives with a care plan that they would adopt him. He had two older half-brothers in the same placement who were going to be subject to special guardianship orders to the same carers. The courts held that Liam's need for stability and security outweighed any perceived advantage to him of maintaining a legal relationship with his half-brothers. He would benefit from the ongoing relationship in living with them, but also needed a legal relationship with his carers.

Re B (A Child)(care proceedings) [2018] EWCA Civ 20: The Court of Appeal upheld a judge's decision to grant a placement order on a child where the plan was to place her with the adopters of her older brother, despite the positive assessment of a paternal cousin and his wife as potential special guardians. The courts held that the value to the child of growing up with a full sibling was considerable, and tipped the balance in favour of adoption, even though there was no existing legal relationship and the children had not yet met.

Petition for Judicial Review by ABC of certain decisions of the Children's Hearings 31 July 2018 [2018] CSOH 81 P1229/17 Opinion of Lady Wise: A court in Scotland ruled that a 14-year-old boy, ABC, should be able to participate fully in his seven-year-old brother's Children's Hearing. The brother (DEF) was the subject of a compulsory supervision order made by a Children's Hearing, which required DEF to reside with foster carers and imposed restrictions on sibling contact. ABC had asked the Hearing to deem him a "relevant person" in respect of his brother's contact arrangements, a request which was refused. In the petition, Lady Wise concluded that the current test for who is classed as a "relevant person" was not sufficient in ABC's case, and that words should be read into the definition to ensure that ABC was classed as such, and therefore could participate in the Hearing.

Appendix 2
Forms and sample letters

Foster carers – Initial overview for each child

Foster carers receive and "hold" a huge amount of rich information about children and typically, when caring for some or all of the child's siblings, you will have a great deal to contribute to assessments.

Please use the form below to share your observations about each child in the sibling group that you are caring for. You will have observed a lot about each of them and your views will be very valuable for the assessment.

Foster carer's observations of child

Name of child:

Brother/sister of:

1. Please provide an overview of _____'s presentation on placement with you and subsequently. Are there any significant changes that you have observed while caring for _____?

2. Please provide a brief summary of his/her strengths and vulnerabilities. Have you noticed any changes since they came to live with you? In particular, how does the child express emotions and respond to care (attempts to soothe/comfort/show affection/set boundaries)?

3. How does the child's behaviour impact on you and your family?

4. Does he/she talk about his/her parents and family? If so, is there someone they focus on particularly? How do they refer to them – with warmth? Wariness? Indifference?

5. How does he/she cope with contact with family members? It would be useful if you can say who they are and your child's reaction to each one.

© Shelagh Beckett and CoramBAAF, 2021. This form is available as a Word template and can be purchased from CoramBAAF along with all the other forms. Contact pubs.sales@corambaaf.org.uk (see page 155)

Contact supervisor – Observations of contact
Interactions during family contact with parents and between siblings

Please use this form to note interactions between parents and children and between siblings.

Date: Venue:

Names of children

_____
_____
_____
_____
_____

Interactions between parent/s and children

1. How did parents greet each child?
   _____
   _____

2. During contact, was there any evidence of differential treatment (DT) and/or differential affection (DA) shown by parents or adult birth relatives? YES/NO

   If YES, please highlight: first time observed/has been observed occasionally/is observed regularly/is observed in most or all contacts

   DT from _____ to _____

   If YES, please highlight: first time observed/has been observed occasionally/is observed regularly/is observed in most or all contacts

   DA from _____ to _____

3. Brief outline of what was observed:
   _____
   _____

Interactions between siblings

1. If the children arrived at different times, how did they greet each other?

2. Outline who interacted and played together. What evidence of fun and shared enjoyment did you observe and between whom?

3. Does one or more of the children tend to lead or dominate?   YES/NO
   If YES, who:

4. Were there any instances of one child helping or comforting a sibling?   YES/NO
   If YES, who:

5. Were there any instances of one child physically hurting a sibling?   YES/NO
   If YES, who:

Name: Role:

Signature: Date:

Foster carers – Observations of contact between separated siblings

Whether you are involved throughout the contact or see children before and afterwards, you are likely to pick up some cues from what a child says or from how they behave.

Please note your observations of contact below:

Names of children

_____
_____
_____
_____

Date of contact _____ and for how long _____

Where contact took place _____

Who attended _____

Your involvement (please tick)

☐ attended throughout

☐ attended part of contact (please outline): _____

☐ took child to and/or collected from contact

Your observations

Please provide notes so far as you are able:

How did the child seem prior to seeing their siblings? (Tick whichever descriptions apply)

☐ appeared to be content / happy / fine

☐ appeared to be no different to usual

☐ appeared to be wary / upset / anxious

☐ other: _____

If you were present, outline how the children interacted (for example: who played together, examples of shared fun and any difficult behaviours or fall-outs)

_____
_____

How did the child seem after contact? (Tick whichever descriptions apply)

☐ appeared to be content / happy / fine

☐ appeared to be no different to usual

☐ appeared more excitable than usual / was upset / was more defiant

☐ other: _____

Any other issues or comments you would like to note

_____

_____

_____

_____

Name of foster carer _____ Signature _____

Date _____

Foster carers – Observations of sibling relationships
Positive and negative aspects

Please use this form over the next two weeks to note interactions between the children as they arise on a daily basis. Your observations are an important part of this assessment.

There is space for recording both positive and any negative or concerning aspects of behaviour between the children. Use as much space as you need under each of the headings. Please use the first name of each child when describing interactions between two or more siblings.

If you notice any patterns or things that you think might "trigger" some behaviours, please make a note of this. We will discuss your observations and thoughts about each child as well as how they get on with each of their siblings. Thank you in advance for your help.

Positive aspects

What examples of positive, pro-social behaviours can you identify in the way that the children interact? Please describe and give examples, and specify the frequency and between whom, e.g. how often actions or behaviours occur, such as: daily/weekly/less often.

Helping

Approximately: daily/weekly/less often

Teaching/encouraging learning – showing a sibling how to do something

Approximately: daily/weekly/less often

Having fun together

Approximately: daily/weekly/less often

Affection shown between siblings

Approximately: daily/weekly/less often

Companionship and spending time with one another, e.g. sitting on sofa together to watch TV

Approximately: daily/weekly/less often

Child showing empathy or understanding towards a sibling

Approximately: daily/weekly/less often

Seeking or giving comfort, e.g. going to sibling when upset

Approximately: daily/weekly/less often

Being loyal or protective – sticking up for sibling if being told off/in trouble/upset

Approximately: daily/weekly/less often

Sharing – sweets, drinks, crisps, time, toys, taking turns

Approximately: daily/weekly/less often

Missing a sibling and looking forward to seeing them (e.g. at the end of a school day)

Approximately: daily/weekly/less often

Any other observations

Identify any examples that you think are positive or that the child might see as positive. Remember that some behaviours that you might think are inappropriate may have been viewed as "good behaviours" within the child's family of origin, for example, a child who has helped look after younger siblings may have had this behaviour reinforced as positive by parents or by the child being placated, smiling, stopping crying, etc. Think about what might have started the behaviour and why it might still be going on.

Negative/difficult aspects

What examples of negative or difficult behaviours can you identify in the way that the children interact? Please specify frequency and between whom, e.g. how often actions or behaviours occur – such as: daily/weekly/less often.

Ignoring another sibling's efforts or requests to play/interact/help

Approximately: daily/weekly/less often

Verbal aggression or threats

Approximately: daily/weekly/less often

Criticising, making negative comments about a sibling, belittling or "putting them down"

Approximately: daily/weekly/less often

Trying to control/dominate, e.g. always or often telling a sibling what to do or how to do something

Approximately: daily/weekly/less often

Scapegoating and unfairly blaming, e.g. one child is often excluded from a sibling group game or always blaming one child for something that they have not done

Approximately: daily/weekly/less often

Do siblings unite to "gang up" against adults/other children? If yes, who?	Yes/No
Is refusal to share with siblings so marked that it worries you?	Yes/No
Do any of the children show frustration that a sibling/s won't leave them alone? If yes, who?	Yes/No

Physical aggression

Tick any of the following that happens, then note between whom and specify the approximate frequency – daily, weekly, less often.

Behaviour	Between _____ and _____	Frequency
Hitting		
Pulling		
Kicking		
Shaking		
Spitting		
Pushing		
Fighting		
Pinching		
Throwing		
Scratching		

Outline the main behaviours that concern you:

_____
_____
_____
_____

Any other observations:

_____
_____
_____
_____

Thank you very much for your time and help.

© Shelagh Beckett and CoramBAAF, 2021. This form is available as a Word template and can be purchased from CoramBAAF along with all the other forms. Contact pubs.sales@corambaaf.org.uk (see page 155)

Children's physical aggression towards others
(Handout for foster carers)

Around half of all parents describe some form of physically aggressive behaviour occurring "sometimes or often" for children as young as 12 months of age. Children aged two and three years show significantly more physically aggressive behaviour than younger children. Physical aggression usually decreases between the ages of three and four years, but may be replaced by other forms of aggression, such as verbal aggression (Alink *et al*, 2006).

In early childhood, most children start to learn to control their behaviour and to regulate their anger and other emotions. They begin to understand more about other people having feelings too. As a result, they learn to respond in a socially acceptable way instead of acting aggressively. The growth in language skills may also help as children develop the ability to verbally communicate many of their needs and wants. Children who struggle to manage their emotions and to communicate their needs may become more frustrated and this may show in angry behaviour. As you will know, most children show some physical aggression to their siblings but this may be at a level and intensity that worries you. It is important that we know about aggressive behaviours that concern you.

Temper tantrums are quite common in early childhood and need not be included in sibling assessments. The main focus is on aggressive acts that may harm another person.

Behaviours that are physically aggressive:

- Hitting
- Pulling
- Kicking
- Shaking
- Spitting
- Pushing
- Fighting
- Pinching
- Throwing
- Scratching
- – or physically threatening any of these.

Behaviours that are not physically aggressive
(if not accompanied by any of the behaviours above)

- Throwing a ball or other appropriate use of toys
- Grabbing or trying to grab an object
- Resisting or trying to "escape" physical restraining
- Dropping something without throwing
- Undirected kicking of the legs or swinging of the arms
- Disobedience, rowdiness, hyperactivity, or anger
- Aggression aimed at the child's own body

Reference: Alink LR, Mesman J, van Zeiji J, Stolk MN, Juffer F, Koot HM, Bakermans-Kranenburg MJ and van IJzendoorn MH (2006) 'The early childhood aggression curve: development of physical aggression in 10- to 50-month-old children', *Child Development*, 77:4, pp. 954–66, see p962

Foster carers – Identifying difficult patterns of behaviour and aggression

Below is a form that can be used to record difficult behaviours, identify conflicts or lack of co-operation between siblings.

Names of children

Sibling conflict topic	Definition	Between whom? Instigator if clear Frequency: daily/ weekly/ occasionally?
Physical	Physical aggression between them (e.g. hitting, scratching, biting, throwing things)	
Verbal	Screaming, yelling and threatening comments exchanged between them	
Teasing	Teasing comments and insults	
Telling tales	How one of them is always "telling on" the other sibling to their parents/carers, etc	
Control	How one sibling is always telling the other sibling what to do or how to do something One child's inappropriate behaviour (e.g. lying, talking back to carers, etc)	
Sharing common objects	Difficulty sharing objects common to both siblings such as a computer or the television, or that one child is always monopolising family items	
Personal objects	Difficulty sharing personal possessions such as comics or bikes, or that one child will take the other child's personal possession without asking the sibling	

© Shelagh Beckett and CoramBAAF, 2021. This form is available as a Word template and can be purchased from CoramBAAF along with all the other forms. Contact pubs.sales@corambaaf.org.uk (see page 155)

Sibling conflict topic	Definition	Between whom? Instigator if clear Frequency: daily/ weekly/ occasionally?
Friends	Difficulty sharing friends, acting differently around friends, or teasing the other in front of friends	
Rejection	One child not wanting to play with another child or rejecting the other child	
Privacy	Wanting to be left alone or having little personal space because of the sibling	
Competition	Do any of the children always need to be "top dog" in games, sports, etc?	
Rivalry – birth family	Do any of the children feel they are being treated better or worse by their parents?	

Any other difficult behaviour that concerns you? Please specify.

Thank you very much for your time and help.

(Adapted from Shirley McGuire, Beth Manke, Afsoon Eftekhari and Judy Dunn)

Parents and relatives – Views about the children and their sibling relationships

For social workers to complete in discussion with each parent, seeking their views about their children's sibling relationships.

For example, you could use the form below. It has some key "starter" questions you might use with the children's mother. "A" is used for the first child subject to this assessment, "B" for the second, and so on for each child subject to this assessment.

Was A a planned child?

How did you feel when you were expecting A?

How did A's name get chosen?

What was life like for you around the time of A's birth? How easy/difficult was it for you?

How did A respond to the birth of B? Did A like to help, like to hold B? Or did A not take much notice of B? (And similarly, for each subsequent child born into the family unit)

How did B's name get chosen? Was he/she a planned baby?

What five words would you use to best describe A?

What five words would you use to best describe B?

© Shelagh Beckett and CoramBAAF, 2021. This form is available as a Word template and can be purchased from CoramBAAF along with all the other forms. Contact pubs.sales@corambaaf.org.uk (see page 155)

What about their father – how do you think he would describe A? And how might he describe B?

_____

_____

Who shared a bedroom? Was this by choice or not? How did it work out for each child?

_____

_____

In what ways is A like you? In what ways is he/she different?

_____

_____

Using five words again, how do you think A would describe B?

_____

_____

If B could talk, how do you think he/she would describe their older brother/sister?

_____

_____

How did A and B each cope when C was born? and so on.

_____

_____

Build on the trigger questions above until you have an initial overview for each child born into the family.

You can use extra copies of this form for other children in the sibling group if it is a large one.

Name	Role
Signature	Date

FORMS AND SAMPLE LETTERS

Parents and relatives – Exploring siblings' roles and any differential treatment of children

For social workers to explore with birth parents/relatives the different roles that the children might have within the family, as well as any differential treatment they may have been subject to.

Key questions to think about might include some or all of the following:

In some families, boys are treated differently to girls – what was it like in your own family when you were growing up? What is important/what is it like in your family now?

As a mum/dad, how do you want your boys to grow up? How do you want them to be? What is important/what is valued in your family?

As a mum/dad, how do you want your girls to grow up? How do you want them to be? What is important/what is valued in your family?

Some people think that boys need to be tough to cope: that by the time they start school they should be able to fight back if someone hurts them. What do you think? What about girls, is it the same for them or different?

Some people say that if you are too soft with boys it just makes life harder for them later on, like when they start school. What do you think?

Is it good to treat boys and girls the same? Or is it better to treat them differently in some ways?

In some families, girls might be expected to do more to help around the house. What do you think is best?

In some families, girls help more with looking after younger ones. In other families it's more about age, the older ones help with the younger ones. What do you think is best?

Who is most like you in your family? In what ways?

Some children might show you that they want kisses and cuddles, for example, they might climb up on to your lap or reach out to you. Who is most likely to want cuddles from you?

Some people think that girls are easier to parent than boys – what do you think?

Some parents get on best with their sons/best with their daughters. What's it like in your family?

Some parents get on best with one of their children. What about you – is there someone that you feel really close to in your family?

How do you know when your child, A, is upset or feeling sad? Do they show how they are feeling?

How do you know when your child, B, is upset or feeling sad? Do they show how they are feeling?

How do you know when your child, C, is upset or feeling sad? Do they show how they are feeling?

How do you know when your child, D, is upset or feeling sad? Do they show how they are feeling?

How do you know when your child, E, is upset or feeling sad? Do they show how they are feeling?

Sometimes the eldest child is the one who likes to "boss" the younger ones around a bit. Did this happen much at home?

Name   Role

Signature   Date

Sibling assessment: key elements
(for social workers)

Think about how you will structure your assessment: what information and observations you might contribute directly and what contributions you can seek from others. The assessment report will include information that has already been obtained. The headings below are intended to provide a guide to key elements that you might helpfully and commonly include and some of which you will already have access to.

- **Details of each child in the sibling group**, including age, gender, ethnicity and current placement.

- **Details of social worker** – qualifications and experience, length of involvement with the children and family.

- **Work undertaken to complete the report**, including dates of interviews and observations, key reports read and supporting evidence obtained from other people.

- **Key background information and impact on children's sibling relationship** – give a brief summary of what led to the children coming into care; what were the supportive factors as well as the adversities experienced? Have the children always lived together? If not, give dates of any periods of separation from their siblings and how their relationship was maintained during these times. What is known about how these experiences have impacted on each child and on their sibling relationships?

- **The views of parents and significant relatives** about each child and their sibling relationship. Highlight the different roles the children may have had in the family and any differential treatment and affection they were subjected to and how that impacted on the children's relationship.

- **Key observations of the children and their sibling relationship** – from all relevant professionals (for example, to include foster carers/current carers; contact supervisors; health and education staff).

- **Findings from SDQ** if completed, and any possible future implications.

- **Overview of each child and their individual needs** – describe and consider each child's needs (identity, developmental, emotional, behavioural, social, health, and education) and highlight any differences in behaviour/presentation observed in different settings or by different people. Consider the implications of these needs for those caring for the child in the future.

- **Overview of sibling relationships** – describe how the children get on together now, any roles they have within the group, the strengths and vulnerabilities of the relationships, and how all of this impacts on each child. Include each child's views about their brothers and sisters, whether expressed directly or as indicated by their behaviour towards one another.

- **Support or interventions provided re: the sibling relationship** – what impact has this work had? Is there any outstanding work that has been identified?

- **Consideration of realistic placement options.**

- **Analysis and recommendation re: placement** – provide your analysis of all information gathered, including any relevant research considered, how this has led to your recommendation/s for future placement of the children, and your reasons for this plan. Is there any significant disagreement about the plan from parents, carers or other professionals and, if so, how has this been taken into account?

- **Consideration of and recommendations for contact** – set out possible options for contact, including the purpose, benefits and risks of each option and what support would be needed. What contact is being recommended and how will this be supported and reviewed?

- **Recommendations for future support** – what work is being proposed to support the children's sibling relationships now and in the future? What support may be needed for the children's long-term carers or adoptive parents, and how will this be provided?

- **Signatures and date report completed.**

Plan your assessment, such that on completion it will include information from a range of sources and people. You may decide to use or adapt some of the forms in Appendix 2, or you or your local authority may decide to develop your own. CoramBAAF has published the Sibling Assessment Report (Form SAR, 2021), developed by Shelagh Beckett and Elaine Dibben (Adoption Consultant, CoramBAAF) and piloted with seven local authorities.

Education – Observations of child

Understanding each child's behaviour and presentation in different settings is an important component of the assessment. Staff in playgroups and other pre-school settings are likely to have a detailed knowledge of the child as well as how he or she relates to other children, similarly for teaching staff working with any school-aged children. The formats below can be adapted but provide a starting point for gathering information.

PRE-SCHOOL: OBSERVATIONS OF CHILD

I would very much welcome your observations and ask you to ascertain and include the views of any other key staff who know the child well. It will be helpful for me to obtain a rounded picture with regard to the child's presentation during structured activities as well as social/play time such as lunch and breaks. The following headings might be helpful:

Name of child:

- Start date

- How long have you known the child?

- How many sessions a week does the child attend and for how long?

- Are there any issues re: attendance?

Overview of the child, strengths and needs
Brief overview of the child when they commenced at the playgroup/nursery and any significant changes you have seen during the child's time in this setting

- What are the child's strengths, talents and interests? Are there any things that the child particularly enjoys?

- How well does the child manage age-appropriate living skills such as toileting and eating?

- Are there any areas of delay/vulnerability/concern? Does the child have any difficulties with learning?

- Are there any issues around how they manage their emotions e.g. dealing with frustration, worries or concerns, getting hurt or upset? Are they able to seek and use the support of adults at these times?

- Do you have any observations regarding the child's placement, i.e. how he/she seems in the foster home (or placement with relatives)?

© Shelagh Beckett and CoramBAAF, 2021. This form is available as a Word template and can be purchased from CoramBAAF along with all the other forms. Contact pubs.sales@corambaaf.org.uk (see page 155)

Relationships here

- With staff – does the child comply with expectations and appropriate adult authority?

- With peers – how well does the child get on with others here? Are there any concerns about bullying or attempts to control others?

Family relationships: current and future care

- Do you have any observations regarding the child's relationships with sibling/s (for example, does the child make comments about them? If so, whom and in what context? Have you seen the child with any of his/her siblings, e.g. when dropped off or collected?)

- Does the child refer to anyone else in his/her family? If so, whom and in what context? Any comments about parents and/or wider family?

- Do you have any comments about what the child hopes might happen in the future?

- Any other observations?

Many thanks for your time and help.

Name   Role

Date

SCHOOL: OBSERVATIONS OF CHILD

I would very much welcome your observations and ask you to ascertain and include the views of any other key staff who know the child well. It will be helpful for me to obtain a rounded picture with regard to the child's presentation in school during lessons and during social/play time such as lunch and breaks. The following headings might be helpful:

Name of child:

- Start date

- How long have you known the child?

- Are there any issues re: attendance?

Overview of the child, strengths and needs

Brief overview of the child when he/she started at the school and any significant changes you have seen during the child's time in this setting

- What are the child's strengths, talents and interests?

- How well does the child manage age-appropriate living skills such as toileting and eating?

- Are there any areas of delay/vulnerability/concern? Does the child have any difficulties with learning?

- Are there any issues around how they manage their emotions e.g. dealing with frustration, worries or concerns, getting hurt or upset? Are they able to seek and use the support of adults at these times?

Relationships here

- With staff – does the child comply with expectations and appropriate adult authority?

- With peers – how well does the child get on with others here? Are there any concerns about bullying or attempts to control others?

Family relationships: current and future care

- Do you have any observations regarding the child's placement, i.e. how he/she seems in the foster home (or placement with relatives)?

- Do you have any observations regarding the child's relationships with sibling/s (for example, does the child make comments about them? If so, whom and in what context? Have you seen the child with any of his/her siblings, e.g. when dropped off or collected?)

- Does the child refer to anyone else in his/her family? If so, whom and in what context? Any comments about parents and/or wider family?

- Do you have any comments about what the child hopes might happen in the future?

- Any other observations?

Many thanks for your time and help.

Name   Role

Date

© Shelagh Beckett and CoramBAAF, 2021. This form is available as a Word template and can be purchased from CoramBAAF along with all the other forms. Contact pubs.sales@corambaaf.org.uk (see page 155)

Observations by health staff

Health professionals often have considerable experience and knowledge of children's early experiences within the family home and important information about how siblings were treated by their parents. Obtaining this can help you identify and evidence some patterns of interaction and how these might have begun, for example, perhaps the children's father favoured boys in the family whilst daughters were treated less well. Health visitor records may provide a rich source of information about how children were treated and how they progressed.

You can use the letter below, adapting as necessary, to send to the health visitor. Remember to mark it confidential, and that your email is secure.

Sample letter

Date:

Dear Health Visitor

I am the social worker for xxx and x.

As you probably know, they came into the care of the local authority and we are now making permanent plans for their future. One of the difficult decisions we have to make is whether the children are likely to do best if they are all placed together or in a particular combination: for example, sometimes with a group of four, it may be that the children might do best in pairs. It is our usual practice to plan for contact if children cannot be placed with all their siblings.

Given the importance of these decisions, I would very much appreciate any helpful observations you are able to provide, in particular the following aspects.

Based on your contact with the family:
Please highlight any significant points for **how each child was treated within the family** – including any differential treatment by parent/partner – please provide brief examples and approximate timing for your observations:

Your observations – **how the children got on with each other** – citing any **positive behaviours** you observed (such as one child showing emotional warmth, helpful or protective behaviours). Please provide brief examples and approximate timing of when you noted this:

Your observations – **how the children got on with each other** – citing any **negative behaviours** you observed (such as one child belittling, hurting or hitting a sibling). Please provide brief examples and approximate timing of when you noted this:

Thank you very much for your time and help.

Yours sincerely

Name: Title:

Appendix 3
Useful reading and online resources

Useful reading

Books on siblings

Argent H (2008) *Ten Top Tips for Placing Siblings*, London: BAAF

Saunders H and Selwyn J with Fursland E (2013) *Placing Large Sibling Groups for Adoption*, London: BAAF

Saunders H and Selwyn J (2011) *Adopting Large Sibling Groups: The experiences of adopters and adoption agencies*, London: BAAF

Books on assessment

Amende E and Patterson L (2015) *Ten Top Tips on Devising a Care Plan*, London: BAAF

Beesley P (2015) *Making Good Assessments: A practical resource guide* (3rd edn), London: CoramBAAF

Cousins J (2011) *Ten Top Tips for Making Matches*, London: BAAF

Books on contact

Adams P (2012) *Planning for Contact in Permanent Placements*, London: BAAF

Argent H (2004) *What is Contact? A guide for children*, London: BAAF

Beek M and Ward E (2015) *Contact After Adoption: A longitudinal study of post-adoption contact arrangements*, London: BAAF

Bond H (2007) *Ten Top Tips for Managing Contact*, London: BAAF

Fursland E (2011) *Foster Care and Social Networking: A guide for social workers and foster carers*, London: BAAF

Fursland E (2011) *Social Networking and Contact: How social workers can help adoptive families*, London: BAAF

Fursland E (2013) *Facing up to Facebook: A survival guide for adoptive families* (2nd edn), London: BAAF

Furland E (2013) *Social Networking and You: A guide for children*, London: BAAF

Macaskill C (2002) *Safe Contact: Children in permanent placements and contact with their birth relatives*, London: Russell House

Neil E and Howe D (2004) *Contact in Adoption and Permanent Foster Care: Research, theory and practice*, London: BAAF

Neil E, Beek M and Ward E (2013) *Contact After Adoption: A follow up in late adolescence*, Norwich: Centre for Research on Children and Families, UEA

Neil E, Beek M and Ward E (2015) *Contact After Adoption: A longitudinal study of post-adoption contact arrangements*, London: BAAF

Neil E, Cossar J, Jones C, Lorgelly P and Young J (2011) *Supporting Direct Contact after Adoption*, London: BAAF

Centre for Research on Children and Families (2014) *The Contact After Adoption Study: Stage 3 of a longitudinal study of adoptive and birth families*, Norwich: Centre for Research on Children and Families, UEA

Books on life story work

Camis J (2001) *My Life and Me*, London: BAAF

Hammond S and Cooper N (2013) *Digital Life Story Work: Using technology to help young people make sense of their experiences*, London: BAAF

Maye J (2011) *Me and My Family*, London: BAAF

Ryan T and Walker R (2016) *Life Story Work: Why, what, how and when*, London: BAAF

Shah S and Argent H (2006) *Life Story Work: What it is and what it means*, London: BAAF

Books on direct work with children

Corrigan M and Moore J (2011) *Listening to Children's Wishes and Feelings: A training programme*, London: BAAF

Corrigan M and Moore J (2011) *Listening to Children's Wishes and Feelings: Course handbook*, London: BAAF

Gilligan R (2009) *Promoting Resilience: Supporting children and young people who are in care, adopted or in need*, London: BAAF

Luckock B and Lefevre M (eds) (2008) *Direct Work: Social Work with Children and Young People in Care*, London: BAAF

Moore J (2012) *Once Upon a Time: Stories and drama to use in direct work with adopted and fostered children*, London: BAAF

Stringer B (2009) *Communicating through Play: Techniques for assessing and preparing children for adoption*, London: BAAF

Books on attachment and the Secure Base model

Cairns K and Cairns B (2016) *Attachment, Trauma and Resilience: Therapeutic caring for children* (2nd edn), London: CoramBAAF

Schofield G and Beek M (2014) *Promoting Attachment and Resilience: A guide for foster carers and adopters on using the Secure Base Model*, London: BAAF

Schofield G and Beek M (2014) *The Secure Base Model: Promoting attachment and resilience in foster care and adoption*, London: BAAF

Schofield G and Beek M (2018) *The Attachment Handbook for Foster Care and Adoption* (2nd edn), London: CoramBAAF

Other books

Cousins J (2008) *Ten Top Tips for Finding Families*, London: BAAF

Dunbar L (2009) *Ten Top Tips for Making Introductions*, London: BAAF

Moffat F (2012) *Writing a Later Life Letter*, London: BAAF

Sayers A and Roach R (2011) *Child Appreciation Days*, London: BAAF

Online practice resources about contact after adoption

The UEA website contains a wealth of useful material: www.uea.ac.uk/contact-after-adoption/home

Online practice resources: http://contact.rip.org.uk/

Siblings, Placements and Contact, Community Care podcast, available at: https://www.ccinform.co.uk/learning-tools/siblings-placements-and-contact-podcast/

Neil E, Beek M and Schofield G (2020) *The UEA Moving to Adoption Model: A guide for adoption social workers, fostering social workers and children's social workers*, Norwich: University of East Anglia, Centre for Research on Children and Families

Neil E, Cossar J, Lorgelly P and Young J (2010) *Helping Birth Families: Services, costs and outcomes*, London: BAAF

Neil E, Cossar J, Jones C, Lorgelly P and Young J (2011) *Supporting Direct Contact after Adoption*, London: BAAF. See also www.adoptionresearchinitiative.org.uk/study5.html

Neil E (2017) *Helping Birth Parents in Adoption: A literature review of birth parent support services, including supporting post-adoption contact*,

Munich: Deutsches Jugendinstitut, available at: www.dji.de/fileadmin/user_upload/bibs2017/Neil_Helping_birth_parents_in_adoption.pdf

The **Research in Practice** website – Fostering and Adoption section (http://contact.rip.org.uk/) provides a useful overview of contact issues. These learning resources were commissioned by the Department for Education in 2013, with the aim of bringing together research and evidence on key aspects of supporting looked after children. The materials are designed to support individuals and learning and development leads to build skills and knowledge for practice and Continuous Professional Development in this area.

Signpost: Topic 15: Managing risks and benefits of contact (the section in respect of after adoption contact with siblings)

Siblings Together
www.siblingstogether.co.uk
Siblings Together is a UK-based charity that promotes positive contact between brothers and sisters separated in foster care, kinship care, residential care or adoption. Services include a Buddy Project and residential camps for looked after siblings aged 7–18 years which aim to provide opportunities for siblings to share experiences that they can cherish.

Stand Up For Siblings
www.standupforsiblings.co.uk
Stand Up For Siblings is a Scotland-wide collaboration between child welfare, children's rights and legal organisations and academics. It aims to value, protect and promote the well-being of brothers and sisters who become looked after or who are at risk of this happening. The organisation aims to influence the law, policy and practice.

STAR
www.siblingsreunited.org.uk
Siblings Reunited (STAR), an initiative based in Fife, reunites siblings who have been separated in the care system, through adoption or kinship care. It provides an opportunity for quality and regular sibling contact, positive shared experiences and a safe, fun learning environment where children can foster emotional bonds and help overcome the trauma associated with separation.

Appendix 4
Adopters' accounts

Various accounts are available on adoption websites and may be useful for you to review occasionally as a resource to use in preparation of prospective families, for example, First4Adoption and Adoption UK.

Whilst separation will be the right choice for some children, the following articles highlight some of the emotions and issues that adopters and their children faced in after adoption contact. The first article also raises issues about preparing children.

Peter and Simon adopted three siblings: Ryan, Lucy and Kelsey

(As told to the author)

Peter and Simon highlight that things may turn out differently compared with difficulties that they and others might have anticipated. As a couple, their relationship with each child can differ and sometimes one child may feel more rewarding than another! They also describe some of the issues that arose for each of their children as their thinking and feelings towards their birth mother change over time.

> Things have been really pretty straightforward for our son, Ryan, who was seven when we adopted him. Interestingly, he was of an age where people would often feel that they are "too old" or that it would be difficult to influence them. This has been the complete opposite for us. Ryan has grown from being in a behaviour support unit, being removed from class for bad behaviour and a difficult child to foster prior to his adoption to now being a committed and talented studious teenager achieving some A*s in his recent exams. He is a well-mannered and very loving young man. We had a few blips in the early days and it sometimes felt like it was difficult to get a message through to Ryan but he now has a clear plan for his future and puts every effort into achieving that. He has learned that not being automatically talented at something is not a reason to give up, and he has seen first-hand the benefits of sticking at things. Ryan has told me that the best thing we have shown him is how to see the funny side of things, and have a laugh! Ryan was extremely close to his birth mother and came to us with a sense of guilt surrounding him not being able to continue to be there for her. One thing he said very early on was that he was 'Sorry but that he would always have to love his mum a bit more than us'. We approached this by making him realise he had permission from us to feel whatever he wanted to feel and no-one could tell him who to love or how much to love them. It was OK to love someone and that didn't mean you had to love someone else a bit less to love a new person. Interestingly, of the three children Ryan has grown far

less close to his mum over time and has developed a relationship on his own terms and this has diminished in significance to Ryan over the years.

Kelsey is a very confident and funny young lady. Whilst my partner will see Kelsey as cheeky or pushing the buttons, I see it in a very different way and believe she is building her character. Kelsey was the youngest in her school year and I think that is difficult for an adopted child. She was far from ready to start school when she came to us yet within a couple of weeks had started the first year of school. From day one she struggled academically and yet she is so very, very bright. In high school this started to have some negative outcomes. Kelsey is extremely popular at school and can mix with a broad range of people; however, more and more she gravitated towards the under-achieving students and those who had problematic home lives. Many of her friends would visit us and get encouragement and time, and Kelsey could relate to their experiences from her own early days. At the same time, she could see other friends achieving academic success and felt more and more distanced from them, starting to create a worrying view of her own academic potential as being significantly less than it was...her aspirations could not have been lower. She was receiving continuous negative comments from school so we made the big decision to move her.

Her new school is fantastic and offers much smaller class sizes and a completely different ethos in which she has absolutely flourished. Whilst her previous school was very highly regarded, it was a large school and it was not meeting Kelsey's needs. She recently got an A and said to me that she was proud of herself and said 'Dad, I know you always thought I could, but I never ever thought I would get an A in anything in my whole life, but I have'. She has a lovely group of friends and has great career prospects. Kelsey had a poor relationship with her mum but out of the three children has developed the closest relationship since adoption. She can see the difficulties her mum faces and she has a good sense of context around this.

Lucy is the youngest and is a very complex little girl. Although Lucy only spent the first year of her life with her birth mother, this time was key; her mother's life was at its most chaotic and we feel Lucy has been affected by this the most out of all three children. She could not speak when she joined us at three and she had been separated from her older brother and sister, Ryan and Kelsey. Lucy has a very close relationship with my partner, but sadly less so with me and there are probably a number of factors around this. We continue to try to improve this. There is an almost unbelievable difference between Lucy's behaviour at school and at home. Although she can be very loving, her behaviour at home is extremely challenging and on some days it feels too much. Lucy is moving on to high school from September and she is very, very excited about this and the fantastic opportunities it offers. We really hope that the benefits we have seen for Kelsey will be replicated for Lucy also.

Emily's relationship with her brother

(Written by Karen Lomas, accessed on BAAF website, 2014)

Karen Lomas adopted her daughter Emily when she was seven years old. Here she recalls Emily's frustration and anger at being separated from her brother. You can read more of Karen's and Emily's reflections on adoption in the book I wish I had been born from you (Lomas, 2009, published by BAAF).

> The day after our adoption had become legal, I met my daughter Emily at the gates of her primary school. On this day there was no greeting, no kiss, no cuddle from my usually affectionate girl but what I can only describe as an "explosion" of the worst fury ever: 'If they wanted me to be specially looked after, don't they know that my brother did that for me and my sisters, and he can still do that? Those stupid people!'

> On and on she yelled. Her arguments were clear, reasoned and extremely well-articulated – she hated, with a passion, the social workers she thought had taken her away from her beloved brother and sisters. I felt impotent in the face of her rage. I also felt that what she was saying made a lot of sense.

> Her anger did eventually abate, although she is still given to rants from time to time. Yet the vital importance of her siblings, especially her brother, was something I understood even more acutely on that day; a day, it should be said, when everything was sealed and our daughter was secure in the knowledge of the legally binding commitment we had made to her. Thus she felt safe enough to give full vent to her anger for the very first time. Until that point, all her energies had gone into ensuring that we were hers and that we would not reject her and send her away.

> In the early stages of the adoption I was unable to relate her personal history to close family and friends without becoming tearful about the enormous loss she continued to feel, particularly with regard to her separation from her siblings. Emily still struggles a great deal to cope with the acute pain she feels as a consequence of living without her brother and two sisters.

> Her yearning for her brother is stronger than anything. After a few months have gone by without contact, Emily's mood fluctuates and she often cries to see him. She misses him desperately and pines before our very eyes. Her frustration and anger at the situation naturally focuses on us, although she knows intellectually that we are not responsible. She is getting better at trusting that we do all we can. Emily is desperate to be with her brother, despite being happy and loved within our family, and we ensure she has regular contact, which now includes regular reciprocal visits. In some ways this appears to have helped Emily and in other ways it has increased her longing to be with her brother on a permanent basis. What is amazing, however, is that she says she would not live with him if she could because she would miss us!

Keeping the sibling bond

(Written by webadmin978, accessed on BAAF website, 2014)

Today we hear from an adopter who has adopted two brothers and talks about the importance of keeping in contact with their four other siblings who have been adopted by another two families...

The decision to adopt siblings was a very easy one to make for me personally. I had always known I wanted a big family and despite a few setbacks, adoption was definitely the way forward. During initial telephone discussions with adoption agencies, each would ask about how many children we wanted, as well as what age and gender. I actually hadn't realised you could adopt more than one child so it was exciting to think I could have two at once!

During the assessment process we talked lots about meeting the needs of two vulnerable children and thought about ways in which their traumatic pasts may impact on their sibling relationship. We also discussed cases where siblings are separated and what type of contact may be in place.

After what seemed like forever, we were finally approved for two children, of either gender, between the ages of 0–5. Thankfully it was not long before our social worker visited us with the profile of two little boys. The first photo we saw of them showed them sitting within a group of four other children – their siblings. My first thoughts were that they all looked lovely and sweet, but my attention remained well and truly focused on the two little boys that I hoped would become mine.

Two weeks later, we found ourselves sat in a matching meeting and watching a video of the boys. It had been taken by the foster carers and showed all the children together. Again, it was clear to see what beautiful children they all were and it was obvious that they all got along well. We were told around this time that the plan would be for all the children to have direct contact twice a year. This sounded fine, although I admit to thinking I would have agreed to anything to get those two little boys because by now I was head over heels in love with them.

Four months after first seeing their photo, I was sat on the foster carer's sofa waiting for them to enter the room. Josh walked in first, quickly followed by Callum and they were everything I had dreamed of. We spent an hour playing before our time was up and we had to leave.

Day two of introductions was emotionally hard. This was not because of Josh and Callum, but because their other siblings were present. It was at this point that it really hit me who these other little people actually were – they were my children's brothers and sisters. They had lived together all their lives and it really was clear now just how strong the bond was between all of the children. We spent three hours there that day and as I left I made a silent promise to my children that I would do everything in my power to make sure they always kept in contact with their siblings.

The rest of introductions went well and as each day passed I got to know Josh and Callum that little bit more. I also built up a lovely relationship with all of the other siblings too. After two weeks, Josh and Callum came home to us, their forever family.

Thankfully over the following two months, the other children also moved on to their forever families.

After three months the first direct contact was planned. It was agreed that the first one would be supported by social workers and after that we (the three adoptive families) would arrange them ourselves. It was a little uncomfortable at first as we tried to manage the children's questions, behaviour and confusion – as well as getting to know the other adults – the mums and dads of my children's siblings. As time went on the children played and appeared to reconnect with each other appropriately. It was a success!

The next contact was arranged by one of the other mums which went very well, and was followed by another a few months later which also went brilliantly. What happened after that is just so natural it is hard to explain. It probably started with one sibling inviting the other siblings to her birthday party, then there was a fun day we all decided to go to, then an invite round to play – before we knew it the two times a year contact had turned into about eight! As families we all got on very well and it felt only natural to invite each other to special events like christenings and birthday parties.

Josh and Callum have been with me for nine years now and although our journey has been somewhat of a rollercoaster due to their early traumatic experiences, the one thing that has always worked well is the sibling contact.

It is a sad fact that many sibling groups need to be split up. This can be for a variety of reasons, such as the sibling group being too big for one family to take on, because the needs of the children mean they could be better off separated, or purely because a permanent family cannot be found for children as a group and separating them would make this possible. Either way, the decision is rarely taken lightly. However, one thing I think is often dismissed too quickly is the issue of direct sibling contact. I have known sibling who have lived together for two, three or more years and are then adopted into different families with an agreement of once a year letterbox contact. In my opinion, this is not fair and certainly not respectful of the children's feelings or relationship with each other.

My two sons needed to be separated from their brothers and sisters because as a group of six they would never have found a family. However, despite this they have never actually lost their siblings. To this day they maintain a fantastic relationship and one that we hope will continue into adulthood.

And then there were two

(Taken from Ashton L (2008) *Take Two*, London: BAAF, pp 129–30)

On 25 December 2006, we were a couple with a promise of an adopted child. Exactly one year later, our parents came – as grandparents – to spend Christmas Day with their children and their children's children. We were suddenly – very suddenly – a family of four and life was so hectic we hardly had the chance to appreciate our new status. We are in an unusual situation: Amber and Emily not only came to us in quick succession, but came like a pair of candlesticks, a matching set. We joke that we have our supermarket children – buy one, get one free. And we didn't have too much time to wonder whether or not it was really a good idea. Emily had been asleep on the dining room table in Sue's house the first time we visited Amber at home. And, at least subconsciously, she had become part of our family when her older sister did. This makes it easy for us to prepare and deliver life story work. We can talk to them together, often when they're in the bath, telling them the story of three little sisters. They will always have the same blood, the same history, and the same concoction of tummy and forever mummies and daddies.

On a different level, I ask myself if this makes them exclusive. They have, in some ways, something that David and I will never share with them: they have each other as full blood relatives. But it is too simplistic to think that way: they have a full blood older sister whom they never see, while Amber mimics me, sounds like me and increasingly looks like me. Interestingly, the absence of the older sister, Katie, makes Amber the older child, a role she fills fully and with verve. I am not sure she would have made such a good middle child. Moreover, Emily is the image of Katie, while she and Amber look only vaguely alike. So they are related, but I'm not sure how significant that is. What makes me happy is that my girls share the same life story and do not have to face it alone. So whenever they reflect on being adopted, or feel the need to search out their birth parents (although we'd be happy to help them there), they can share any fear or anxieties with one another. They are a protective mechanism for each other, should they need one. They come from exactly the same mould. In that sense, they are very lucky sisters.